Elijah at the Wedding Feast and Other Tales

Stories of the Human Spirit

John Shea

ACTA

ASSISTING CHRISTIANS TO ACT

PUBLICATIONS

Elijah at the Wedding Feast and Other Tales
by John Shea

Edited by Gregory F. Augustine Pierce
Cover Design by Tom A. Wright
Text design and typsetting by Garrison Productions

Acknowledgements for the use of copywritten stories is listed on page 153. Any failure to give proper credit or obtain needed permissions for the use of stories in this book are inadvertent and will be corrected in future editions.

ISBN: 0-87946-207-8

Library of Congress Catalog Number: 99-65631

Printed in the United States of America

03 Year/Printing 8 7 6 5 4 3

Contents

To the stories my mother told

and

the story my mother is.

Introduction

The Window and the Mirror

People say to me, "I need a story that will inspire me" or "I need a story that will calm me" or "I need a story that will make me believe in people again" or "I need a good laugh. Got anything?"

The stories here may inspire and calm. There may even be a tale or two that can call people back from the land of cynicism. Of course, I hope laughter happens. However, I do not know which stories will do what. I cannot predict responses. These stories seek to evoke the human spirit, and spirit cannot be predetermined. Matching story with response leaves out surprise, and surprise is the calling card of spirit.

People not only seek stories for themselves and their moods. They also want stories for other people. They ask, "I will be working with teenagers. Do you have any stories about teenagers?" Or they say, "I have a session with senior citizens. Do you have some good stories that deal with aging?" Or they want to know,

"Do you have some stories that explore the ups and downs of trying to be a parent?"

In the stories in this book, teenagers, elders and parents all make appearances. But I would suggest telling teenagers the stories about elders and parents, and telling elders the stories about teenagers and parents, and telling parents the stories about elders and teenagers. And the other stories in this book...tell them to whomever will sit still long enough to listen. Do not predetermine who will hear which story.

Although we instinctively try to match story with audience, this matching is often very superficial. It presupposes that people are only interested in someone like themselves—someone at their age or in their situation. Over the years, however, I have learned to trust stories, especially stories that have spiritual ambitions or struggle to communicate spiritual wisdom. Tell any story and people with "ears to hear and eyes to see" will make the story their own. They will place its wisdom into the cinematic flow of their lives.

In fact, it is often helpful if the story begins by not being about them at all. When we carefully match story and audience, people have their defenses up. Teenagers know more about being a teenager than any dorky storyteller. Parents are quick to point out that parenting is more complicated than the story implies. Elders smile at the presumption of any storyteller who tries to get their experience right. Whenever a story is supposedly about them, listeners do not relax. They sit back, fold their arms, and say, "Show me."

When a story initially appears not to be about them, however, defenses are down. It is about a cigar smoker, and I do not puff; a gold thief, and I am an honest citizen; a nun, and I am a Protestant; a tailor, and I am a sailor; two brothers, and I am an only child; a child on a farm, and I grew up in Manhattan; a Jew attending services with his son, and I am a Hindu. Since the story is not about the listener, there is no need to be on guard.

As Murray Krieger pointed out, a story begins as a window. We are looking into the lives of others, into a world with which we are not familiar. In the course of the story, however, the window turns into a mirror. People who are not us show us to ourselves. We see ourselves in what is happening in others' lives.

This "seeing ourselves" usually happens fast. We grasp the connection in a flash. Then comes the moment of decision. Either we turn away and pretend we did not see what we saw, or we host the wisdom of the story into our lives. If we decide to host it, we have moved from "story time" to "chewing time," from hearing the story to puzzling its wisdom into the nitty-gritty of our lives. If we manage to do this even in a modest way, we have received the blessings of the story.

The stories presented here seek to be blessings in the lives of the readers. The book is a motley collection of tales. Some are revered stories of spiritual traditions, some are mere anecdotes, some are personal experiences told in story form. They have all been crafted, however, to communicate spiritual wisdom. In other words, they want us to see our lives as the spiritual adventures they are.

On the cover of this book, Elijah whirls around. Inside is the story of how this whirling teaches the wedding guests the truth of their celebration. Join them.

The Belt Buckle

It happened in Oklahoma City when I was a young man, fresh on the speakers' circuit. I had just finished my talk, and people were coming up to ask me questions or point out things I should have said.

An old Native American man—a Cherokee, I suppose—suddenly stood in front of me. He had a large and elaborate belt buckle in his hands. It was a swirl of multicolored beads. If they formed a pattern, I couldn't detect it.

"Please accept this gift," he said.

I was a little taken aback, but I had a quick response: "Thank you. It's beautiful. But I can't accept it."

"Why not?" he asked with a puzzled look.

I pointed to the expanse beneath my chest. "Well, would *you* want to call attention to *this* stomach with a large, beautiful belt buckle?" I laughed.

The man did not smile. He simply extended the belt buckle again. "Please accept this," he said again.

"It's too expensive," I said. This was probably closer to the truth of why I said no. I was always taught not to take expensive presents from people. The belt buckle was hand-crafted and had a look of elegance about it.

"You know," the old man said, "*you* can give it to someone *else.*"

I accepted the belt buckle.

Eventually, I followed the old man's advice and gave the belt buckle to someone else, a student whom I thought had made excellent progress.

The student said he couldn't take it.

I told him the story of how I had received it, and then he took the belt buckle with a knowing smile. Although we did not discuss it, I am sure he knew the gift was to be given away. It was not a possession but a mission.

Spiritual teaching often targets possessions for special consideration. Better said, it focuses on why and how we hold onto things. Sometimes the teaching has a social edge—prophetically pointing out that a few people have many things and many people have a few things. The goods of the earth are unequally distributed, and the people with much will not let go and share with the people who have little. Why is this so, the spiritual masters ask. Why do we continue to accumulate abundance and turn away from the outstretched hands of those with not enough?

But at other times, the teaching on this subject is directly theological. It uncovers the idolatrous dynamics underneath the grasping for things. In a fearful, panicky, yet never totally conscious place inside ourselves, we think possessions will make us secure in what is basically an insecure existence. On one level, of course, this perception is relatively accurate. Accumulating money and land *does* make people more secure than those who do not have these things. On a deeper level, however, we all know that possessions cannot stop the ravages of time or the arbitrariness of life's events. Only God is a "rock in this weary land." Yet possessions can trick us into thinking they can substitute for faith in God. So we pursue them under false pretenses, thinking we are gaining protection when all we are doing is trading in illusion. This is why a fundamental choice is necessary. "You cannot serve God and wealth" (Matthew 6:24), Jesus taught.

The story of the belt buckle moves us in yet another

direction. It does not force us to look at the terrible gap between rich and poor or encourage us to examine our interior, idolatrous attachments. Instead, it plays on the very boundaries between the physical and the spiritual. The belt buckle, in all its intricately beaded beauty, is a stunning object of the physical world. Therefore, the Law of the Closed Hand is operative. That is, if my fingers are around it, it is mine.

This Law of the Closed Hand has a strong hold on many of us. It never even dawned on me that I was to give the belt buckle to someone else. That had to be pointed out to me with a gentle insistence. I thought that if I took the gift it was going to be mine, to be thrown in a drawer with all the other "things" that I possess. But then I was taught a law from the spiritual realm: A gift is meant to be given away. If the physical world works by the Law of the Closed Hand, the spiritual world works by the Law of the Open Hand.

At one point in St. Matthew's gospel, Jesus instructs his disciples: "You received without payment, give without payment" (Matthew 10:8). I have always been struck by the depth of consciousness this saying reflects. It does not talk of obligation or gratitude or the responsibility attendant on possessions. It makes no rational argument for the better distribution of goods. There is no appeal to guilt. Jesus simply wants us to acknowledge a flow, a connection between receiving and giving, that is natural and free—an abundance of life that cannot be

hoarded. The proper response to gift is to participate in it with freedom, not to possess it out of fear.

This spiritual dynamic is subtly initiated by the act of
receiving. When someone freely offers an unde-
served or unexpected gift, we often push it away
because we cannot make it fit into our conventional
mind-set of how things work. On the surface, we
have a supply of good reasons for resisting. (Why
advertise my belly? It is inappropriate to take an expensive gift from a stranger.) On a deeper level, however, we probably surmise that we are being drawn
into a process that will change the way we do business—a crazy process grounded in truths that un-
dermine the dominance of the Law of the Closed
Hand.

Once we receive the free gift, we are automatically
commissioned into the world of giving. We begin to
operate by the laws of the spiritual world within the
life of the physical world. While one hand still closes
around things, the other hand begins to open to others.

Today, tonight, tomorrow, soon...someone is moving toward you with a beautiful beaded belt buckle.
He or she will not take "no" for an answer.

The Cigar Smoker

The cigar smoker was giving a workshop in Los Angeles. It began in glory and ended in humiliation. At the close, people were grumbling, and his departure was more in the nature of an escape. But as the cab dragged through traffic to the airport, he thought to himself. "If only I can get to the airport, get on the plane, nurse a double martini, eat whatever lousy food the airline is serving, and smoke my cigar, everything will be all right." (For this was many years ago, when cigar smoking on airplanes was allowed.)

For the first time in three days, there were no hitches. He got to the airport, got on the plane, and plunked himself down in an aisle seat in the smoking section.

Next to him in the middle seat was a little girl, around four years old. She had with her everything little girls carry on airplanes—a half-eaten bag of Fritos, a coloring book with a box of broken crayons, and a doll, mussed from too much hugging and squeezing. In the window seat sat the little girl's mother.

Los Angeles, as usual, was socked in, a thick mixture of fog and smog. As the plane left the ground, it entered the thick, gray clouds. The cabin darkened. But as the plane climbed, the cabin grew progressively lighter until the dazzling moment when the plane broke out of the clouds into the sun.

The captain turned off the no-smoking sign. The woman in the window seat lit up a cigarette. When the cigar smoker looked over and saw her, his heart sank. As she exhaled the smoke, she waved her hand back and forth in front of her mouth. The smoke wafted upward and drifted toward the front of the cabin.

The cigar smoker instantly knew what this meant. This woman was going to smoke her cigarette, but there was going to be no smoke in the little girl's eyes. But the cigar smoker also knew that when he lit his cigar, smoke would swirl through the cabin, infiltrate the cockpit, and seep out into the universe. And if he lit his cigar, this little girl would be engulfed in smoke. She would be coughing her pathetic little-girl cough. People would be staring angrily at him. He would be the bad guy of all time.

The cigar smoker folded his arms and allowed the injustice of it all full reign over his soul. His thoughts boiled.

Did he not get a seat in the smoking section? He did.

Do they allow you to smoke cigars in the smoking section? They do. (Or at least they did!)

Does he need a cigar? Oh sweet Jesus, he needs a cigar.

Will he be allowed to smoke a cigar? He will not.

He sank sullenly into the seat and entertained the idea of locking the little girl in the washroom.

The woman in the window seat finished her cigarette and said to the little girl, "Jennifer, come here." She helped Jennifer slide over and sit on her lap. "Jennifer," the mother instructed her, "look at the clouds."

Jennifer looked out the window of the airplane and looked *down* at the clouds. The little girl immediately began to sob and repeat in a frightened voice, "We're upside down! We're upside down!"

The cigar smoker turned toward the noise and coolly observed the little girl's panic. He thought to himself, "All her life, this little kid has been standing on the ground looking up at the clouds. Now she is over the clouds looking down. She naturally thinks she is upside down." But he decided that it was not his place to say anything.

Jennifer's mother was the soul of logic. She explained to her, "We are in an airplane, Jennifer. When you are in an airplane, you go up in the air. When you go up in the air, you go over the clouds. So, you see, we are not upside down. We are right side up." And then from the mother's mouth came a conclusion that she was obviously not prepared to admit but which she could not avoid. "The clouds are upside down."

To which Jennifer replied, her sobs deepening, "We're upside down! We're upside down!"

The mother pressed the button for the cabin attendant; and down the aisle came a trained and confident stewardess, prepared for any eventuality.

She leaned over the cigar smoker and said in a syrupy voice to the little girl, "What's your name?"

"Jennifer," the girl whimpered.

"What's the matter, Jennifer?"

"We're upside down."

"No, we're not, honey," the flight attendant assured her. Then she talked about her experience of flying and that sometimes she gets afraid too, but that really there is nothing to worry about because the captain knows what he is doing, and what she finds often helps is some Coca-Cola and some peanuts, and that she was going to get some and bring them back to her, and then she would see that there was no reason to cry.

The cabin attendant retreated down the aisle, smiling.

Jennifer sobbed, "We're upside down! We're upside down!"

Jennifer's mother, leaving reason, resorted to discipline. She picked the little girl off her lap and planted her firmly back in the middle seat. "Sit there and be good," she warned.

Jennifer sat there, holding her thin knees and making soft crying noises that anyone with ear to hear could pick up.

The cigar smoker heard. He leaned over to the little girl and said, "Jennifer, you are upside down!"

The little girl looked up at him in grateful recognition.

"But it's O.K." said the cigar smoker. "It's O.K."

Jennifer climbed over the arm of her seat and sat in the cigar smoker's lap, and for a moment, before her mother could rescue her, for one dazzling moment comparable to when an airplane breaks out of the darkened clouds into the sun, the cigar smoker knew he really didn't need the cigar.

When there is no change in your circumstances, how can there somehow be a change in you? When you are still upside down, how can it be "O.K."? If you are still being unfairly deprived of your cigar, how can it suddenly become no big deal?

This human possibility is often called the "transformation of meaning." Our perceptions and attitudes are so closely tied to our experiences that when those perceptions and attitudes are changed the experience itself is transformed. Changing how we look at things is one way we adapt and cope. If we think being upside down is O.K., we relate better to the experience than if we think being upside down is threatening. If we understand that our not smoking made possible an unexpected yet satisfying human contact, our sense of deprivation is not as strong. We may even come to the realization that we "really didn't need the cigar."

When these insights happen, the outer world remains the same. We, however, inhabit it differently, so its meaning changes.

Working with our inner attitudes is usually not our first choice. Being "somewhere else" is what we desire. If we are in physical pain, we want it to stop. If we are without a job, we want to get one. If we are in a bad relationship, we want out. If we are upside down, we want to be right side up (and everyone will do their best to convince us that we are). If we are without our cigar, we want to be puffing on it...now. Common sense tells us this is how to proceed: Bolt! Stop the suffering! Seek the desired situation!

"The Cigar Smoker," however, considers another way, a way we usually only back into when there is no escape from the objective state of affairs. Only then do we contemplate the possibility of some inner re-working. For example, I was told the story of a woman who was sick in bed. When she was asked how she was doing, she replied, "I would rather be here than anywhere else in the world." This woman does not desire anything different than the life she has. Therefore, although she may be in pain, she is not suffering. As the Buddhists insistently point out, suffering stops when desire ceases.

"The Cigar Smoker" ends with Jennifer and the sto-ryteller both wanting to be where they are at that moment. They have changed, even though their cir-cumstances have not.

I do not know how to evaluate this human capacity to transform situations by changing their meanings and adjusting our attitudes. I do not know when we should move in this direction and when it would just be a cop-out, when we are exercising a pro-found human option for inner peace and when we are merely giving up too soon.

However, I do know that it is better to be aware of the path of meaning transformation than to be igno-rant of it.

The Couple Planting a Tree

A spiritual master and a disciple were walking down a road in a rural section of the country. As they walked, they were discussing the deeper meaning of life: Why are we here? Why is there something and not nothing? What should we strive for? When everything dies, does anything matter?

As they turned a bend in the road, they saw an old couple out in a field. The couple was packing soil around a fledgling tree they had just planted. The disciple saw the incongruity of what they were doing and commented, "Master, here is an example of what we are talking about. These old people are planting a tree they will never live to see grow. Is not all experience like this?"

The master replied, "Ask them why they plant a tree they will never see grow."

The disciple pushed out into the grassy field, talked to the old couple for a moment, and returned to the road.

The master asked the disciple, "What did they say?"

The disciple had a puzzled look. "They said, 'The good is enough.'"

In *How I Believe,* Teilhard de Chardin constructed an argument about our deepest desires. It was not a logical *tour de force* that sought to constrain his readers' minds along his path of thinking. Rather, it asked us to look into ourselves and see what Teilhard was sure was already there. Although I have never been fully convinced by his effort, I have always been enticed by it and return to it often.

Teilhard begins by describing an elementary psychological fact. While he admits it takes some training of the "inner eye" to perceive this fact, he is sure it is present in all people. He argues that we undertake every true act (defined as an act in which a person gives something of his or her own life) out of a drive to construct a "work of abiding value." There is, he says, an essential instinct in us that makes us guess "at the joy, as the only worthwhile joy, of cooperating as one individual atom in the final establishment of a world: and *ultimately nothing else can mean anything to me.*" Later, Teilhard characterizes this drive as a passion to "release some infinitesimal quantity of the absolute, to free one fragment of being."

Really, Teilhard? I hadn't noticed that releasing some infinitesimal quantity of the absolute is what is ultimately driving me.

Teilhard's friends had the same reservations as I do. They wrote off his inner explorations as his need to philosophize. He quotes them as saying, "We simply get on with our work and studies because that is what we like doing, just as we like having a drink." But Teilhard came back at them, "You are not searching to the full depth of your heart and mind. And that, moreover, is why the cosmic sense and faith in the world are dormant in you. You find satisfaction in the fight and the victory, and it is there that the attraction lies. But can you not see, then, that what is satisfied in you by effort is the passion *for being finally and permanently more?*"

Quite frankly, most days I cannot fathom what Teilhard is talking about, but sometimes I get a glimpse. He writes with such passion and certitude that I feel I am in the presence of a consciousness that is both more expansive and more nuanced than my own. He sees the human essence with a clarity of which I am not capable. I know he is not referring to ego fantasy—the sick ambition, born of an internalized shame, to be God, to have arbitrary power over everything. Rather, Teilhard is pointing at *contribution*—the drive to give ourselves and our lives to what is absolute. "Man," he writes, "the more he is man, can give himself only to what he loves; and ultimately he loves only what is indestructible." At a deep level of our being, we want to construct what Teilhard calls a "work of abiding value." What he is saying, I think, is that everything we do, everything we really put ourselves into, has this desire built into it.

I believe Jesus promised that this spiritual passion in us would be fulfilled. In one episode, the disciples return from their travels rejoicing. They tell Jesus that they have expelled demons—the forces that degrade and destroy the human (see Luke 10: 17-20). Jesus compliments them but ends his response with the admonition, "Nevertheless, do not rejoice because demons are subject to you but because your names are written in the sky." For Jesus, expelling demons is not a sign of individual power. It is a participation in the divine mission of liberation and, as such, enters into the reality of God and God's work. The disciples' names are written in the sky—in other words, their work transcends time and contributes to abiding values.

But how can this be? Time is the Great Devourer. Things we did yesterday are forgotten today. Things we do today will be forgotten tomorrow. Walk the cemeteries and observe the absence of fresh flowers on old graves. How do we contribute to a work of abiding value when nothing abides?

People speculate on how this happens. Maybe all we do that coincides with the values of God is taken up into God and stored in "everlastingness." Or perhaps every act of self donation becomes a stone in the building of the house of the world. Possibly, at some future time and in the light of some future fulfillment, what we all contributed and how all things worked together for good will be evident. Then we will see how all of who we are and what we do is a sacrifice into the ongoing life of the world. Nothing will have been lost. No genuine effort will have been in vain.

Until that time, there is trust. Trust always combines a not-knowing with an enthusiastic doing. For example, I do not know how the pages of this book, which contain something of my own life, contribute to a work of abiding value, but I write them with trust nevertheless. Nor do I know how visits to the sick, making meals for those we love, caring for the young, struggles for justice, tears of remorse, eight-hour workdays, and all our other small and great endeavors survive the unfolding of time within the fading memory of human history.

Yet, on my better days, I engage with gusto, opening myself to a mystery more beautiful and more subtle than I comprehend. I do want to awaken what Teilhard thinks might be dormant in me—a cosmic sense and faith in the world.

I will not see the trees I plant grow completely. No one will. Yet the planting is good.

And the good is enough.

Elijah at the Wedding Feast

E lijah was not only the muscular prophet of the Hebrew Scriptures. In legend and lore he also became a trickster and a bit of a magician.

Elijah roamed the world precipitating situations that would bring people to deeper understandings. Because he never completely discarded his prophetic mantle, these situations often included a certain amount of healthy confrontation. He held up a mirror to people. Some had the courage to look. Many did not.

One day Elijah was walking down the street. From behind the outer wall of a house he thought he heard the sound of a party. Party-prone as he was, Elijah was about to knock on the door to see if a friendly host might invite him in, when suddenly a deeper scheme occurred to him.

The prophet spun around and was suddenly clothed in the rags of a beggar. From toe to top his clothes were torn and tattered. Elijah rapped upon the door, and a man opened it and looked at him. "I was just outside," Elijah began, oozing as much charm as is possible for a prophet of the Most High, "and I thought I heard the sound of a party. If this is true, I was wondering if there might be room for one like me."

The man looked Elijah up and down, and the look in his eyes was *not* one of approval. "You are correct," the man said with disdain, "It is the wedding of my daughter, and the feast is flourishing, but for one such as you there is no room."

The door slammed in Elijah's face.

Elijah then took three steps back and spun around a second time. The rags of a beggar magically became the fine garb of a gentleman. He was about to knock on the door a second time when he realized that something was missing. He snapped his fingers and there appeared in his hand a fine wooden cane with a gold handle. Elijah rapped upon the door with the cane.

The same man opened the door and looked Elijah up and down. "I was just outside," the prophet started, his opening memorized, "and I thought I heard the sound of party. If this is true, I was wondering if there might be room for one like me."

The man gazed at Elijah in his fine clothes. "Well, sir, you are correct," the man said. "It is the wedding of my daughter, and the feast is flourishing, but for one such as you there is always room."

Elijah was ushered in. This time, the door slammed behind him.

At the feast there was a long table, sagging with food. The guests milled about, helping themselves to this delicacy and that sweet morsel. Elijah advanced to the table, prowled up and down, then suddenly scooped a handful of food and stuffed it in one of his pockets. Some of the guests saw this and stepped back.

Elijah took some more food and packed his other pockets with it. More guests stepped back.

Then Elijah began pushing food into his shirt and vest, much of it falling to the floor. All the guests were watching in astonishment and disgust. The host was summoned and came and stood next to Elijah as the prophet took a carafe of wine and poured it over his fine clothes—first over one shoulder, then over the other, and finally down the middle.

"Sir," the host finally said to Elijah, "I do not understand. I invite you into the wedding of my daughter and you stuff food into your fine clothes and pour wine over your elegant attire."

"Well," said Elijah, "It makes perfect sense to me. When I, Elijah, came to your house in the rags of a beggar, I was refused entry. When I, the same Elijah, came to your house in the clothes of a gentleman, I was admitted. I could only conclude that you had invited my clothes to the feast. So I have proceeded to feed them."

The host and all the guests were embarrassed. They looked at the floor. When they looked up, Elijah was gone. All that remained was a fine wooden cane with a gold handle.

"Do not judge by appearances, but judge with right judgment" (John 7:24). As usual, St. John's admonition is correct. But it is appearances that we first see, and appearances have a way of capturing our attention and triggering our judgments. This is the lesson of "Elijah at the Wedding Feast."

Elijah in rags and Elijah in fine clothes was the same person, but he was treated quite differently based on his appearance. Getting past the repulsion of poverty and the allurement of riches is no easy task, even today. We are often caught in the trap of evaluating people on how they look, and that is just the beginning of our "pre-judge-tice."

When our dalliance with clothes and accouterments is finished, our dalliance with bodies begins. Our culture has determined that some bodies are "beautiful" and some are "ugly." Some are in "good" shape and some in "poor" shape. Some bodies have been twisted by accident and some have been perfected by exercise. Some are young and firm, others are old and flabby. Now, noticing bodies is one thing, but equating person with body is quite another.

Attending to bodies leads inevitably to attending to personalities. One fiction author, for example, his male ego in the ascendancy, wrote this: "Inside her body that would not quit lived the soul of a New Jersey housewife." How Elijah the trickster would have had fun with that writer! Just as clothes come with bodies, so do bodies come with personalities. Personalities are complexes of qualities that both manifest and hide a person. "She is like that," we say, or "You can count on him to react that way." But just like the host in the Elijah story, we can put people in a box from which there is no escape. In truth, although personalities can be typed (and there seems to be endless fascination in doing so), people's personalities are very fluid and capable of almost endless variation and surprise.

However, personality is not the final reality, the final layer of appearance. There is a deeper reality that is not as accessible as the other layers. This reality is the ultimate subject of our clothes, our bodies, our personalities, and it is the reality known best by lovers. I have often thought that love travels a path of interiority. It begins with attraction to clothes and bodies, continues with the slow process of learning personality, and flowers in the realization of person.

It is not easy to discern person. My favorite image of its emergence is from Gerard Manley Hopkins' famous poem in which he describes God's grandeur that "flashes forth like shook foil." I think this same image applies to the child of God in us. It "flashes forth" and is noticed by a couple in love with each other.

When they are operating on this level, for example, her shyness is no longer an imperfection but a quality that merely hides more than it reveals; his sullenness is not a relationship-breaking trait but part of the total package that happens to block more than it mediates. In moments of spiritual awareness, lovers' imperfect clothes, bodies and personalities are integrated into a larger reality of the ever-transcending person that is the beloved. This is at least part of what is meant when we talk of love as a mystery.

Now for the best part.

Once lovers have caught a glimpse of the ever-transcending person that is the beloved, there is a path of return. They have journeyed into the spiritual center of the other, and now they must journey out. Going in entails discernment, getting past the various outward appearances. Going out entails allowing the mystery of the other person to suffuse personality, body and clothes.

The best word for what happens in this going out process is "radiance." An inner radiance lights up the entire reality of the beloved, and the lover's only task is to receive it.

That is why Elijah teaches this truth at a wedding. It is at the level of person that people marry, and it should be at the level of person that they are invited to the feast.

The Evangelizers at the Beach

Years ago, I was lying on the North Avenue beach in Chicago in the late afternoon. The sun was beating down on me when all of a sudden a shadow blocked the light. For a moment I thought it was a passing cloud, but then I opened my eyes and there were two young people standing over me.

They were well washed and groomed. He had on a white shirt and a tie, and she wore a blouse and a skirt. They were carrying their shoes, and they each had a Bible in hand.

They looked down on me and asked, "Do you know the Lord Jesus as your personal savior?"

I looked up and answered without missing a beat, "Unfortunately, yes."

There have been many creative responses to unwanted evangelizers. Annie Dillard was once accosted by a fervent ten-year-old who asked her, "Do you know Jesus as your personal savior?" She responded, "I also know your mother." (Turns out, the mother had recently asked Dillard the same question.) When Fitz Perls was confronted with the question, "Have you been saved?" he shot back, "I'm trying to figure out how to be spent." So people have learned to hit the initial intruding volley of fundamentalists back over the net.

My come-back in this mini-story, however, was not said in irritation or meant to be a clever put down. The young people's interruption of my sun worship stunned me into a real response. It just came out. I realized that I do know Jesus as my personal savior, but there is a bittersweet quality to the relationship.

Of course, there is a great deal of difference between what they mean by "Jesus as a personal savior" and what I mean. Not that my perceptions and feelings about Jesus as savior are normative or even laudable. My attitude witnesses to the place where I am, not the place where I should be or even the place where I will be sometime in the future.

For me, salvation refers to the process of consciously engaging in the dynamics of spiritual living. It is both an invitation and a process. We can refuse the invitation and that is the end of it. (In gospel imagery, the birds of the air have flown away with the seed, and the earth—which is us—does not get a chance to bring forth fruit.)

We can also accept the invitation. When we do that, we begin a journey, but it is a journey we may not finish. (The seed sprouts up but has no roots and withers under the sun, or thorns grow up and choke it.)

The optimal scenario proposed by the gospels is to accept the invitation and then to navigate the full process. (Then the seed will bring forth fruit—thirty, sixty, a hundredfold.) It has been said about the spiritual life, "Better not to begin. But if you begin, better to finish."

I came in contact with the gospels as a young person. I heard the invitation and set forth for the feast. The birds of the air did not fly away with the seed, nor have roots withered or thorns choked—at least not completely. Still, I cannot claim that there has yet been an abundant harvest in my spiritual life. To employ another gospel image, I seem always to become detoured on the road to the banquet. Delay and diversion are spiritual tactics I know well.

Many years ago, when I realized how wayward my wanderings would be, I wrote this:

But, brother and sister, we both dimly see
   the struggle is the goal
   the search is what we know.
All the rest is heaven.

This is the gist of my "Unfortunately, yes" response to the evangelizers on the beach. It was not a theological argument but a gut reaction based on my own experience. My acceptance of "Jesus as my personal savior"— which is just as real as (even if totally different from) these young people's—has left me permanently unfinished, completely dependent on mercy, turning always toward a Source I cannot fully know and a neighbor I cannot full trust. The truth is, Jesus walks too fast. As St. Mark describes anyone who would dare to be a disciple, "They were on the road, going up to Jerusalem, and Jesus was walking ahead of them; they were amazed, and those who followed were afraid" (Mark 10:32).

I can relate to this fear. It seems to me that the mind and heart of Christ is always more than we can comprehend and bear. Salvation lies in our stumbling along after him. Lately, I have been stumbling along after an appraisal of Jesus by St. Matthew. He borrows a phrase from Isaiah to describe the Master: "He will not break a bruised reed or quench a smoldering wick" (Matthew 12:20). I interpret this to mean that if a reed was so badly damaged that it was almost split, Jesus would not add to the destruction and deliver the final blow. If a wick had lost all flame and was just about expired, Jesus would not finish it off and quench it between his fingers.

There is nothing in Jesus that contributes to death. Even if death is imminent (as with a bruised reed or a smoldering wick), he will not hurry it along. Even in situations of extreme brokenness, Jesus' imagination is completely attracted to the emergence of life, not its destruction.

This is the invitation to which I say yes. No matter how wounded we are, we must not contribute to the woundedness. We must find life in the midst of dying and embrace it. This is the message of personal salvation that emerges for me from the pages of the gospels. But when I try to live it, I find my life characterized by struggle and search.

That is why my "yes" is preceded by "unfortunately."

And it would still be the beginning of any conversation I might have with my young evangelizing friends.

The Gold Thief

There was a man who dreamed of gold. Night after night, he dreamed of gold. Even during the day, gold was continually in his thoughts.

One night, after a particularly long and rigorous bout of dreaming about gold, the man got up and quickly went into the marketplace. There were a hundred people in the marketplace, and the man pushed his way through to the tents of the gold vendor, and on the gold vendor's table was a whole slew of gold earrings, bracelets and necklaces.

The man just took his arm and swept across the table of gold artifacts and pulled them into a bag he had on his other arm and turned around and began to run.

There was a policeman only four steps behind the man. The policeman grabbed him, cuffed him, took him into the police station, and put him in jail.

As the policeman was walking away from the cell, he said to the man, "I don't understand you. What a stupid thief you are! There, in the sight of a hundred people, with the gold vendor right in front of you and me right behind you, you try to steal all this gold."

The man said, "I never saw any of you. I only saw the gold."

In **The Color Purple,** one of Alice Walker's characters, Shug, suggests that God is constantly trying to get our attention. She suggests that is why the color purple exists—purely to get us to notice its beauty. If we fail to notice, Shug assures us, God gets "pissed." When God gets "pissed," however, there is no divine retribution. God merely makes something else in the hope that this new "thing" will cause us to notice and exclaim. The full-time work of God is to attract us to the beauty of the world.

We, unfortunately, have other preoccupations. Our minds latch onto one of God's "things" (like gold) and we obsess over it. It is all we can see. We cannot shake its image from our minds. We acknowledge our imprisonment in simple language: "I never saw any of you. I only saw the gold."

Usually, the things we latch onto the most are our worries. Whatever we worry about so preoccupies us that nothing else can be appreciated. It is in this situation that God gets "pissed" and creates something else to unstick us. And for those of us who can really get mired in our worries, God has to be especially inventive.

One Christmas season, for example, I was deep into obsessing about my seemingly precarious future. I was invited to a party and thought it might help me to "get my mind on something else." However, I was also worried that everyone would ask me how I was doing and, inadvertently, sink me deeper into my other worries. (How's that for piling worry on top of worry?)

After much vacillating, I decided to go to the party. It was in a condominium, so I parked in the basement area and took the elevator up to my friend's apartment. As I got on, I noticed a grocery cart and a mobile clothes rack standing next to the elevator. (Many apartment buildings have these helpful carriers available. People come from the grocery store or the cleaners, open the trunks of their cars, and load the grocery cart with bags or hang their clothes on the rack. They then wheel them onto the elevator, take them upstairs, unload them, and return them to the basement for the next person to use.)

Sure enough, at the party everyone asked me how I was doing, and I responded to their empathetic inquiries. But with every sentence, I sank into deeper and deeper self-absorption. Like the man in "The

Gold Thief," I could see only one thing: my own worries. After four hours of this exercise in self-pity, I took the elevator back to the garage area to get my car and worry my way back home.

As I stepped off the elevator, I heard a loud noise. I turned and looked to my left. The clothes cart was coming toward me, wheeling really fast. At the front of the cart was a girl of about ten, hanging onto the front vertical pole and leaning way forward. She reminded me of Kate Winslet, hanging over the front of the ship in the movie *Titanic*. The Leonardo DeCaprio role, however, was being played by someone quite long in the tooth. I suspect it was her grandfather. He was pushing the cart from behind. Actually, he had one foot on the base of the cart and the other on the cement of the garage floor. He was making the clothes rack move in skateboard fashion, and he had it going fast enough to lift the long, blondish-brown hair of his granddaughter ever so slightly off her shoulders. Both of them were delighting in their play.

As they sped by, I waved.

And suddenly I thought I heard the voice of a "pissed-off" God, a voice that came from the sky but had managed to reverberate in the parking garage, say very clearly, "Well, that got your attention, didn't it, you self-pitying jerk?"

It is the only time God has ever talked to me.

The Grocer and His Parrot

A grocer found a beautiful parrot for sale in the market, and, excited about his purchase, set about installing a hook in the ceiling of his little shop, from which he intended to hang the parrot's cage. He had found the perfect location, too—right in the doorway, where the magnificent bird would be easily visible from the outside. The grocer figured that the parrot, with its colorful plumage and its gift of speech, would attract many customers. The bird would thus be a good investment, boosting business for the shop, which admittedly had not been doing so well lately.

And sure enough, it was just as the grocer had hoped. As soon as the parrot opened his mouth, curious passersby who hear him from outside would enter into the store to listen to the bird's interesting chatter, and would end up buying something out of courtesy. The shopkeeper named the parrot Sweet Tongue. Not only was the bird the star of the marketplace, but eventually he also became a good friend of the grocer himself.

Sweet Tongue was not an ordinary parrot. He seemed not merely to mimic words but actually to understand their meaning. He could hold conversations with his grocer friend and, interestingly enough, listened to the man's daily complaints and offered advice. And despite his name, Sweet Tongue would say anything he liked, whether it was something nice or not. This sort of talk, even if it was a harsh criticism of the human listener, was not offensive to those who were so addressed. As a matter of fact, people accepted the bird's comments in good humor.

The business of the grocery flourished, enabling the grocer to move into a bigger store and expand his inventory. Business was improving so greatly that he added a few displays of herbal medicine to the store. Eventually, after the grocer had invested a large sum of money in the shop, he decided to make a large part of it a complete apothecary. Hundreds of bottles, large and small, containing all sorts of oils and ointments, potions and syrups, went on display.

The appreciative grocer became very fond of his feathered companion and rewarded the bird by letting him fly freely about the store. One morning, as the grocer was unlocking the door to his shop, he smelled a strong aroma coming from inside. Once the door was open, he saw Sweet Tongue flying from one corner to the other, all the bottles had been broken and were scattered on the floor. Apparently, the parrot had hit the bottles while flying and had knocked them over. It is no exaggeration to say that the new apothecary displays were utterly in ruins. A great investment seemed to have gone down the drain.

At first the grocer was in shock. But as the minutes went by and he regained his senses, he became enraged. He seized Sweet Tongue by the throat and hit him on the head so many times that the poor bird almost expired on the spot. Then he threw the bird into his cage and sat down and cried over the misfortune. Hours later, the grocer realized that because he had struck the parrot's head, Sweet Tongue had lost his head feathers. The poor parrot, now totally bald, was confined to his cage once again.

In time, the grocer was able to recover the losses to his business. However, there was one piece of irreparable damage: Sweet Tongue, who now looked rather ugly, had fallen silent after the incident. Naturally the customers who came merely to enjoy Sweet Tongue's chatter and bright appearance stopped shopping at the store. The grocer's business, which had flourished before, began to decline.

The grocer planned various schemes to make the parrot talk again. He tried tempting him with delicious nuts, but the bird showed no interest in such food. Then he brought a musician to the store to play. The music was intended to revive Sweet Tongue's spirit, so that he would forgive the grocer and speak again. But still he remained mute. In a last attempt, the grocer brought a female parrot and put her cage in front of Sweet Tongue's. The grocer told Sweet Tongue that he would set both of them free to fly about the store if only he would talk. However, the bird ignored both the grocer and the female parrot. When the grocer opened the door of the cage and encouraged Sweet Tongue to fly around the shop, the bird squeezed into the back corner of his cage and refused to budge.

Finally, the grocer gave up trying. Resigned to the idea that the parrot had gone dumb after the shock to his body, he left Sweet Tongue in peace. Yet, not totally without hope, the grocer gave alms and said prayers. Perhaps through his piety the parrot would eventually talk again.

One day, a wandering dervish with patched cloak and beggar's bowl was passing by the store. He was totally bald. Suddenly, a nasal voice from inside the store called out, "Hey, you! How did you end up bald? Did you break some bottles, too?"

The bald dervish turned around to see who had addressed him. To his surprise he saw that it was a parrot speaking to him. The grocer, elated by this sudden stroke of fortune, invited the dervish in and explained the story of the medicine bottles and how the parrot had become bald and speechless. The dervish approached the cage and said to Sweet Tongue, "So, you think the reason I am bald is because of a situation similar to yours?"

"What else could it be?" replied the parrot.

The dervish smiled. "My friend, let me give you a word of advice: no two leaves on a tree are the same! Neither are two persons with similar appearances alike, for one person may reflect on his life's experiences while the other remains ignorant. There are many, though, who think that, in fact, the two are alike. How oblivious they are, for there is no disparity greater than that between the wise and the ignorant. It is like the difference between Moses' staff and Aaron's—one has the power of God, the other that of man; one makes miracles, the other magic. Nothing causes more trouble than the human habit of judging things by their appearance, because what might look the same on the surface may not be the same in essence. Take the example of the honeybee and the bumblebee: they look alike, but from one comes honey, while from the other comes pain."

The dervish stopped talking and gave the grocer an insightful look, as if reading his soul. The parrot was now sitting quietly in his cage, and the grocer seemed stunned. The dervish then smiled and, without a work, walked out.

Moments later, when the grocer came to his senses, he realized that such a lesson as he had been given was not to be taken lightly. He ran outside to thank the Sufi. But the man had disappeared, and no one could recall having seen a bald dervish in the bazaar that day.

From *Tales from the Land of the Sufis,* © 1994 by Mojdah Bayat and Mohammad Ali Jamnia, (Boston: Shambhala Publications, Inc., pp. 136-139). All rights reserved.

When I first read this story, I laughed. I knew I wanted to learn how to tell it, but there was one interaction in the story that puzzled me. In fact, it is the key interaction between the dervish and the parrot: "My friend, let me give you a word of advice: no two leaves on the tree are the same!"

Of course, Sweet Tongue starts it when he asks the dervish if his baldness was caused by the same type of mishap that had caused the parrot's own. That supplies the surface connection, but I suspected there was a deeper dynamic at work in the story that was eluding me.

When I started telling the story to people, I began to see what that "more" might be. First of all, people began chuckling right from the beginning. The whole idea of the parrot and the grocer and their personal and business relationship had people smiling. But the sequence that brought outright, prolonged laughter was the grocer's schemes to get Sweet Tongue to talk again. He tries everything: nuts, music, sex. People followed this series of enticements with increased merriment. Nothing works. The stubborn Sweet Tongue remains silent.

Finally, the grocer resorts to everyone's final strategy—our back-to-the-wall, last-ditch effort. He "gave alms and said prayers." And his prayer is answered. The dervish arrives.

When Sweet Tongue finally does talk, he asks the dervish, "Hey, you! How did you end up bald? Did you break some bottles, too?" It is at this point in the story that virtually every audience I have told it to has become convulsed. I think listeners relate to the stubbornness and self-absorption of the parrot. He has been wronged and is going to hang on to his injury as long as he can. The efforts of the grocer at reconciliation and making amends are futile. We have all been there, have we not? We have all been Sweet Tongue, nursing our pain and refusing anything that would call us out of it. There is an undeniably seductive pleasure in being a victim.

Likewise, we have all been the grocer, trying our best to make up for our outbursts and misdeeds and getting nowhere. I believe listeners' universal laughter when Sweet Tongue finally speaks is because the grocer and the parrot have slowly become a mirror in which we recognize ourselves.

This is the context for the dervish's piece of advice. At one level, it is a standard piece of spiritual wisdom: Do not be fooled by appearances. What may look alike to physical eyes may be incredibly different in essence. The parrot should not mistake the dervish's baldness and his own for the same thing. Although they may look alike, "no two leaves on the tree are the same."

But only the ignorant stay on this outer level of appearances. The wise go beneath appearances and reflect on their experience. In doing so they are continually learning, discerning the difference between miracles (Moses' staff) and magic (Aaron's staff) and between honey (the honeybee) and pain (the bumblebee). But it is precisely this that Sweet Tongue has refused to do. He has not learned from his experience. He is still stuck in what has happened to him.

The story does not tell us if Sweet Tongue ever "heard" the dervish's advice, but we have heard it. The question is whether or not we will take it to heart. The grocer apparently has done so. The dervish gives him "an insightful look, as if reading his soul" and the grocer comes to his senses and realizes that "such a lesson as he had been given was not to be taken lightly." The dervish's words have taken him to a space of spirit, and he runs outside to search for the dervish who has blessed him with so great a lesson. But the holy man cannot be found. In fact, no one can recall having seen a bald dervish in the bazaar that day.

Such is the elusiveness of spiritual wisdom.

The Higher Math of Sr. Imelda

S ister Imelda is a retired member of the Adorers of the Infant Jesus. She helps out in the library of an all boys Catholic high school. She is the subject of tales, both true and tall.

Once there was a psychologist who came into the classroom of the senior boys to conduct workshops on "values clarification." One of his exercises was to seat two boys across from each other. On the table between them were two lines of coins. One line contained a quarter and a nickel; the other line had three dimes and quarter. The setup looked like this:

Line One	Line Two
quarter	three dimes
nickel	quarter

The rules were simple. One boy (chosen by lot) got to choose one of the lines. If he chose line one, he got to keep the quarter and the other boy received the nickel. If the chooser picked line two, he kept the three dimes and the other boy got the quarter. The chooser could choose either line of coins, but his counterpart had to take the lower amount in that line.

Seven out of ten of the choosers chose line one.

The psychologist pointed out that this was a somewhat surprising result. Had the choosers taken line two, they would have each received thirty cents—five cents more than if they chose line one. But they would have been only five cents ahead of their rivals across the table. When they chose line one, they had five cents less but were twenty cents ahead of their partners. The psychologist concluded that the boys were not motivated by greed as much as by competition. What they wanted more than money was to be as far ahead of the next guy as possible.

"Huh, wow! That makes you think," said one of the boys, speaking for all. He said it as if it was a new experience.

Just then, Sister Imelda came into the room with a handful of overdue book notices, each containing a fine.

Now, it is the nature of human beings that the moment we learn something new—especially if it has the potential of tricking another human being—we have to give it a try.

"S'ter, S'ter, come here a minute," called Jimmie Ivoniak. "Sit right down here, S'ter. See the two lines of coins. You get to choose. Take the quarter and I get the nickel. Take the three dimes and I get the quarter. Which one do you pick, S'ter?"

Sr. Imelda contemplated the coins for a moment, arched her right eyebrow, and said, "Why don't the two of us take line two together, Mr. Ivoniak? Then we'll have fifty-five cents between us."

For the first time in his young life, Jimmie Ivoniak had nothing to say.

Sister Imelda stood. The boys who had gathered around her divided like the Red Sea as she swept towards the door. Then she stopped, turned, and said, "Even the entire fifty-five cents, Mr. Ivoniak, would not be enough to cover your book fine."

Thus did Sister Imelda clarify the values of the senior class.

Without consulting the dog-eared catechism of my youth, I vaguely remember that actual graces are helps from God that come unbidden. They illumine our minds, inspire our wills, and encourage us to live a better life. I have become a firm believer in actual graces, not because the catechism promotes them but because I cannot seem to avoid them. It seems God wants to help and is very ingenious at finding ways to do it.

In particular, actual graces take the form of words other people say to me. This is not specific advice meant to address some problem. Rather they are random words, words that come out of nowhere, words my family, friends, colleagues, students, even strangers don't know I need to hear. They are unbidden but on target. They tell me a truth I need to hear.

Consider the following interchange. One day I am in my office, stewing about something or other, frantic about my professional future, when the phone rings. A business acquaintance tells me he is going in for tests for colon cancer. He says, "Trusting has always been difficult for me, but there is no other way." I tell the man I will pray for him, but I do not tell him what he had just done for me. As I hang up the phone, my soul is in hot pursuit of the clue he has given me. I suddenly see a way forward out of my dilemma. Even better, his words seem to be a first step on a more peaceful path. "There is no other way"—the right words at the right time, unexpected but exactly what was needed. An actual grace.

I was told a story about a mother who was very upset with her daughter. The mother lived in Minnesota and the daughter was working at a camp for mentally challenged teenagers in New York. The daughter called and told her mother that she was dating one of the counselors. That did it. In the mother's eyes, her daughter had always been trouble—wrong companions, wrong attitudes, wrong boyfriends, wrong this, wrong that. The mother decided to go to New York immediately and—one more time—straighten her daughter out.

On the plane, the woman sat next to an elderly Native American man. Although she wanted to ponder just what she was going to say to her daughter, the man insisted on making conversation. She finally broke down and told him that she was going to see her daughter who was working with mentally challenged teenagers. The man said, "Oh, your daughter is a healer."

The woman now testifies that the man's words allowed her to see her daughter in a whole new light. She was suddenly going to New York not to correct her daughter's mistakes but to be with a healer. The old man's words were an actual grace.

In "The Higher Math of Sister Imelda," the title character is a walking actual grace. She offers a line that Jimmie Ivoniak is not ready for. It is a line, however, that is tailor-made for him and the entire senior class—the offer of cooperation in the midst of competition. "Why don't the two of us take line two together, Mr. Ivoniak?" she asks. "Then we'll have fifty-five cents between us." Sr. Imelda offers a reminder of togetherness in a game where separateness is highlighted. Her comment is unbidden and illuminating.

The story does not tell us what Mr. Ivoniak did after he recovered his tongue. Even actual graces have to be received, taken into ourselves, and pondered. They often sting, and at first they can feel like a putdown. But that is only because we are often attached to destructive ideas and images, and the advent of a new way of looking at things exposes our secret holdings. When we embrace and cooperate with actual grace, however, life unfolds in the direction of redemption.

I have a friend who holds that "when you are in trouble, the whole universe comes to your aid." I can list a million examples that refute that claim. Yet I have learned to be attentive for a grace-filled word—a word I cannot predict and a word I cannot conjure on my own. More often than not, it arrives.

The Holy Shadow

As everybody knows, the Angelic Council meets on Wednesday afternoons from 3:00 to 5:00 to consider earthly candidates for special gifts, rewards and honors. The list of potential recipients is usually long and a lot of "weeding out" is necessary.

It is not generally known, on the other hand, that angels—like most humans—complain about their work. During these Council sessions, there is usually a number of demands for five-minute breaks and a great deal of talk about overwork and burnout.

After one particularly tedious meeting, the potential recipient for the week was selected and the name was sent "upstairs." The Angelic Council, of course, is purely advisory to the Divine Source, who has to give the final O.K. to each nominee. This time, a memo came down that said, "Approved, but ask her first."

The Angelic Council selected a subcommittee. They immediately flew to earth and found their potential recipient. In a formal and solemn presentation, they offered her a gift. "You have been found worthy," they said in unison. (With so much time spent in the angelic choir, angels always speak in unison.) "We are pleased to give you the gift of healing touch. Whomever you lay your hands upon will be healed."

The woman said that she was sure the gift of healing touch was very much needed in the world in which she lived, but she declined the honor. "Perhaps someone else would accept it," she said.

The angels quickly caucused. Being superior beings, they adjusted their plans to meet the situation and returned with a new offer. "You have been found worthy," they said in unison. "We are pleased to give you the gift of conversion of hearts. Whenever you speak, people will be moved to change their lives for the better."

"I am sure that the gift of conversion of hearts is very much needed in the world in which I live," replied the woman, "but someone else must accept that gift. I decline the honor."

Grumbling now, the angels caucused a second time. They returned with a new proposal. "You have been found worthy," they said in unison. "We are pleased to give you the gift of great virtue. People will see your deeds and be encouraged to live lives of high moral values."

The woman agreed that the gift of great virtue was

very much needed in the world in which she lived, but she insisted that someone else needed to receive it. She declined once again.

It was only after the woman's third refusal that the angels remembered what the divine memo had said: "Ask her first."

"So what is it you want?" the angels asked in frustrated unison.

The woman answered quickly, for she always knew what she wanted. "I want the gift of doing good," she said, "but not knowing it."

The angels caucused. This was a new and unforeseen request. They were energized and buzzing with the challenge, their wings beating excitedly. After some time, they came upon the way that the "gift of doing good but not knowing it" could be bestowed.

They made the woman's shadow a source of goodness. She would go about her life doing what had to be done, but whatever or whomever her shadow fell upon would be graced. As she walked by a withered brook and her shadow fell across it, for example, it would suddenly gurgle with sweet, clear, running water. If her shadow fell upon a sullen child, the child would suddenly smile contentedly. If she passed a world-weary man, he would reawaken to vital purpose and passion. And so the woman would live, going about doing good and not knowing it.

The people in her world respected the humility of the woman. They never told her of the healing effects of her shadow, although many tried to walk behind her. And since her good deeds were never explicitly attributed to her, her name has been forgotten.

She is remembered only as the Holy Shadow.

Between soup and salad at a wedding dinner, the man sitting next to me (who had not missed the cocktail hour) told me bluntly, "All religions are the same: Do good and avoid evil." I told him that the mystical strands of religious traditions are leery of people who "do good." The mystics are suspicious of the motives of "do-gooders."

The man obviously did not want the conversation to go in this direction and changed subjects. Earlier in that week, however, a friend of mine who is a life-long spiritual seeker did want to go there. In fact, she brought me there.

She was telling me she had visited a spiritual community that had impressed her greatly. The people in the community exhibited a high level of care and compassion. She had been able to have a long conversation with the founder and guide of the community and told him he should be proud of what he had brought about. He replied, "Everything you see here is because of the grace of my teacher." My friend ended this vignette with, "As you can see, Jack, he is the real McCoy."

It took me awhile to see what she had told me I could see. What she meant was that the leader of the community did not identify with the fruits of his labor. He did not take credit for what happened, even though he was instrumental in bringing it about. This was not false modesty or the obligatory Academy Award "thank you to everyone who made this movie." The spiritual master saw the whole thing from a spiritual perspective. His own mentor had taught him, and he in turn was responding to the grace his teacher had been to him by passing along the teaching and the way of life it promoted. The man viewed himself as a medium of grace—not the doer and claimer of good deeds.

In "The Holy Shadow," the angels consider the rewards of healing touch, conversion of hearts, and great virtue to be the hallmarks of genuine religion, just as my dinner companion associated the ethical slogan, "Do good and avoid evil," with universal religious idealism. Mystical perspectives, however, spy a danger in all human gifts and all human striving. The mystics fear we will not recognize and acknowledge the Divine Source, that we will become obsessed with the proximate players. Then the ego will step forward: "I can heal by touch; I can convert others by speaking; I can gather a following by the power of my example." The tendency to think that our good deeds will make us righteous cuts us off from the source of all goodness and separates us from our fellow human beings. Praising our goodness somehow denigrates theirs.

Although this story is inspired by the Sufi tradition, it would be at home in the gospels. When Jesus told people they were the light of the world, he urged them to let their good works shine forth so that people would see them and "give glory to your Father in heaven" (Matthew 5: 16). Good works are a testament to the goodness of God, not us. In a similar vein, when a man asks Jesus, "Teacher, what good deed must I do to have eternal life?" Jesus shoots back, "Why do you ask me about what is good? There is only one who is good" (Matthew 19:16-17). The retort is clear: Do not associate yourself with goodness. Humans do not possess goodness, they only reflect the goodness of God. And everyone has a chance to do so. Flannery O'Connor once remarked, "When the sun hits the trees a certain way, even the meanest of them sparkle."

Christians are fond of litanies. We line up saints known for their stellar lives and plead with them to both influence God on our behalf and be models for our struggling lives. Perhaps we should add a symbolic name—a name for all the no-name saints, a name for all the forgotten ones who in their time and place allowed the goodness of God to shine forth in the world.

"Holy Shadow, pray for us!"

"How Come I Felt So Bad?"

Y ou never know what questions kids are going to ask, especially when you are putting them down for the night. That is when there is enough of a slow down for them to review the day and pursue what is really on their minds.

As Tom tucked in little Tommy, he felt that tonight his eight-year-old son might want to relive the happy events of the day. Tommy's team had won the little league championship that morning. Tommy had three hits and his friend Phil had hit the game-winning home run.

"Pretty good day," Tom said to Tommy as he sat on the side of his son's bed. But Tommy did not respond. The boy looked pensive.

"Dad, you know when Phil hit the homer and everyone ran onto the field and we jumped up and down?"

"Yeah," said the father, not know where this was going.

"I was happy, but inside I felt sort of bad too. How come I felt so bad when Phil got the winning hit?"

Tom wished that his son had asked him about sex. It would have been easier.

Even the most glib among us, the never-tongue-tied, have been silenced by the heart-felt question of a child—especially when the kid has stumbled upon one of the chronic dilemmas of the human condition.

In this story, the question is: How come the boy feels bad when someone else succeeds, especially when the one who succeeds is his teammate and friend?

If it was someone on the team playing against him who hit the home run, feeling bad might be the proper response. Wallowing in the "agony of defeat" is sports protocol. In fact, in that situation, feeling bad could really be good, because it would show how fierce was his drive to win. "Look how down Tommy is. He really wanted this one!" is high praise in the locker room.

This, however, is the success of the boy's friend and teammate and, by extension, his own success, yet he feels bad "inside." These strange and unwanted feelings are inviting young Tommy into an inner world that could start him on a spiritual path, but his father knows these feelings are difficult to see clearly and untangle. In fact, for most of us having a conversation about sex is easier than talking about feeling bad when you should be feeling good.

Feeling bad when someone else—especially a friend—does good is a confusing experience. When we look at it closely, however, an underlying structure of comparison and competition begins to emerge. When someone else goes "up," in a way we go "down." We discover that competition is not something outside us or restricted to certain activities such as sports. It is deeply embedded in our sense of ourselves. We know who we are by how we measure up. Comparison is how we find our place. As Phil is rounding the bases, Tommy is reduced to a fan.

Even in the middle of friendship, where we least expect it, competitive put-down appears regularly, and the reason we feel bad over the success of another is out in the open: We perceive we are diminished by someone else's excellence. He or she is ahead of us, therefore we trail behind.

Like Tommy, once our competitiveness comes up on our mental screen, we have lost our innocence. We see how pervasive the world of comparison is. It enters our lives very early and continues and intensifies as we grow. We compete for our place in our families, schools and workplaces. It even enters into our love lives: The boy steals the girl from another suitor; the girl dumps one admirer and entices another. Competition is part of the air we breathe.

In this atmosphere, we can easily get locked in on ourselves. Everything is seen from the point of view of our shaky self-esteem. The success and excellence of other people is experienced as a personal put-down. A beautiful house is a comment on the shabbiness of our own abode. An imaginative piece of writing convicts our own prose of dullness. Every smiling lotto winner reminds us just how unlucky we are. In a wonderful phrase, we get "down in the mouth." After a baseball loss, Charlie Brown's teammates huddle around him and offer these words of consolation: "Well, Charlie Brown, you win some and you lose some." Charlie answers: "Wouldn't that be nice." A category forms in our mind, a category we use to sort people, including ourselves, into two groups: "winners" and "losers."

As we grow older, of course, we learn to manage competition in a number of ways. We select what we will compete in and for. We are quick to sense when we are "out of our league." ("How 'bout you and me play some basketball for money?" says the six-foot-six college kid. "I think not," you wisely respond.) We also do our best to keep competitiveness in its place—as a spur to excellence rather then a defining factor of who we are. We learn to admire others for what they can do, rather than begrudge them their success. We find the knob that turns down the volume on the comparison tape that plays continuously in our heads.

Not all of this is possible for eight-year-old Tommy yet. He is just beginning to understand there is both an outer and an inner world of competition and selfhood. If he continues to work with this insight, however, it will become a genuine spiritual path, and he may discover some of the great spiritual truths about it that virtually all religious traditions hold up for us. His consciousness may begin to coincide with a self that is *beyond* competition. He may notice that he can take up an attitude toward his competitive mind and recognize how it both shapes and distorts his life. In religious language, this deeper self is the image of God or the child of God. It participates in the transcendence of God and allows us to be always a little more than what is happening around us.

When Tommy notices his "feeling bad" and asks his father the question "Why," he has already gone beyond the spasm of competition in the outer world and begun to explore his inner world. He is into the transcendent self-beyond-competition and has had a glimpse of the meaning of St. Paul's scolding remark, "When they measure themselves by one another, and compare themselves with one another, they do not show good sense" (2 Corinthians 10:12).

Tommy may someday discover that he loves excellence more than he envies the bearers of excellence. As medieval theologians pointed out, we can come to cultivate a liking for the true, the good, the one and the beautiful—in and for themselves. Once we are grounded in this spiritual appreciation, we delight in the appearance of these transcendental qualities. It does not matter who is their carrier, whether ourselves or others. What matters is their sheer occurrence. We recognize that excellence is not the property of anyone, but anyone can be its bearer into the particularities of life.

Still, as we struggle not to be envious when truth or unity or beauty or goodness suffuses a life that is not ours, there is always a twinge—that ineradicable and involuntary spasm deep within us that signals that we are feeling empty in the presence of fullness, threatened by what we perceive as another's power and good fortune. But if we work at it, we can become old hands at noticing and dismissing these reactions. They are fruitless, simply part of what is unredeemed in us.

A father sits on the side of his son's bed. A question comes between them: "How come I felt so bad?"

Advice to parents is cheap. It never takes into account the moment—how unexpected the question is, how unfair it is for a boy to have a concern he is not yet capable of exploring fully. The parent, by definition, is not ready. He himself has not worked through this problem of the human spirit with anything resembling enough wisdom to pass on to his child. There is nothing for the father to do except relive with his son the moment of excellence, to pull it from their collective memory with pleasure.

The bat hits the ball...the sound of full contact, a delight to the ears...the sight of the ball, climbing and soaring...the left fielder turning in hopeless pursuit...the bases being turned and the crowd cheering joyfully.

How could anyone feel bad?

By the way, it was Phil who hit it.

Mary, Joseph, the Midwife, Salome and the Child

J oseph saddled his donkey and set Mary upon it. They drew near Bethlehem—they were three miles distant—and Joseph turned and saw Mary looking gloomy, and he said, "Probably that which is in her is distressing her."

Once again, Joseph turned and saw her laughing, and he said, "Mary, how is it that I see your face at one moment laughing and at another time gloomy?"

She said to Joseph, "It is because I see two peoples with my eyes, the one weeping and mourning, the other rejoicing and glad."

He found there a cave and he brought her in. Then

he went out to seek a Hebrew midwife in the country of Bethlehem.

Now I, Joseph, was walking about, and I looked up and saw the Heaven standing still, and I observed the air in amazement, and the birds of Heaven at rest. Then I looked down at the earth, and I saw a vessel lying there, and workers reclining, and their hands were in the vessel. Those who were chewing did not chew, and those who were lifting did not lift up, and those who were carrying to their mouth did not carry, but all faces were looking upward. I saw sheep standing still, and the shepherd raised his hand to strike them, and his hand remained up. I observed the streaming river, and I saw the mouths of the kids at the water, but they were not drinking. Then suddenly all things were driven in their course.

Finding a midwife, he brought her. They came down from the mountain and Joseph said to the midwife, "Mary is the one who was betrothed to me, but she, having been brought up in the Temple of the Lord, has conceived by the Holy Spirit." And the midwife went with him.

They stood in the place of the cave, and a dark cloud was overshadowing the cave. The midwife said, "My soul is magnified today, for my eyes have seen a mystery: a Savior has been born to Israel!" And immediately the cloud withdrew from the cave, and a great light appeared in the cave so that their eyes could not bear it. After a while the light withdrew, until the baby appeared. It came and took the breast of its mother Mary, and the midwife cried out, "How great is this day, for I have seen this new wonder!"

The midwife went in and placed Mary in position, and Salome examined her virginal nature, and Salome cried aloud that she had tempted the living God—"and behold, my hand falls away from me in fire." Then she prayed to the Lord.

Behold, an angel of the Lord appeared saying to Salome, "Your prayer has been heard before the Lord God. Come near and take up the child and this will save you." She did so; and Salome was healed as she worshipped.

In the Gospel of Matthew, the birth of Christ is assumed rather than told. It is announced that a child will be conceived and born, and then three Wise Men seek and find him. The story of his birth is not recorded.

In the Gospel of Luke, the actual birth of Jesus is told in two sentences—a highly symbolic two sentences to be sure, but two sentences nonetheless: "While they were there, the time came for her to deliver her child. And she gave birth to her firstborn son and wrapped him in bands of cloth, and laid him in a manger, because there was no place for them in the inn" (Luke 2:6-7).

In the Gospel of James, which did not make it into the official canon of the Church, there is no such reticence. In this story, we are treated to a conversation between Mary and Joseph, a personal witness of Joseph, and a tale of two women.

Many people scrutinize the infancy narratives of Matthew and Luke to uncover historically reliable facts about the birth of Jesus of Nazareth. Although the stories are more theological and spiritual than historical, the fact-finding expeditions show no signs of letting up. In an age when the video camera is the criterion of truth, inquiring minds want to know: What really happened?

Very few people, on the other hand, want to explore the historicity of the Gospel of James. I guess it is assumed that this rendition is historically false just because it is not in the Bible. That is a blessing, however, for it allows us to inhabit its imaginative richness and spiritual symbolism without the distraction of determining what is "true."

In spiritual biographies, birth narratives are often foreshadowings. They augur truths that will be unfolded at length through the person's life. The juxtaposition of Mary laughing and Mary sad alludes to a number of situations still to come. It presages the dual response to Jesus' proclamation and message. Those who receive it will rejoice; those who reject it will be forlorn. It also points to the path of sadness and joy the disciples will walk—weeping at the death of Christ, rejoicing at his resurrection. As St. John images it: "When a woman is in labor, she has pain, because her hour has come. But when her child is born, she no longer remembers the anguish because of the joy of having brought a human being into the world" (John 16:21). There is an inescapable flow of experience in the life of every person. We are all destined to sadness and joy, to a mix of love and loss. The one born of Mary will be our companion in the fullness of what it means to be human.

The next part of the story is Joseph's testimony. (This switch to first-person testimony is jolting from a narrative point of view. However, it probably signifies that what he says is trustworthy.) In Joseph's eyes, the world stops. Birds, people and animals pause. Relentless time abates, and eternity enters. The eternal "now" has stilled everything. "Then suddenly all things were driven in their course." Is it possible that human consciousness can rest in the eternal and then suddenly return to the "drivenness" of time? When all things stop, do we become aware of their beauty in a new way? Does the stopping allow the particularities of life—hands and vessels, chewing and lifting and carrying, open mouths ready to drink—to impress themselves on us? Is eternity the backdrop needed to kiss the fleeting life of time? Is that what Christ will teach in the hills of Galilee and on the streets of Jerusalem?

Next the midwife witnesses the birth. It begins in a cloud of darkness that gives way to an unbearable light which, in turn, withdraws to reveal a child reaching for its mother's breast. These symbols carry the conviction that God is the ultimate author of the birth of this child. At the dawn of creation, God called light out of darkness, and whenever the divine acts, this process is repeated: Darkness is succeeded by a light so blinding that it must recede before human eyes can adjust. What remains to be seen is a child reaching for its mother's breast. "How great is this day, for I have seen this new wonder!" the midwife says. God's ultimate creative act is the person of Jesus.

There is now in the story a final episode of immense significance. The prophetess Salome decides to check out the miraculous birth by giving Mary a gynecological exam. Could this possibly be a virginal birth? Salome's error is that she tries to test the spiritual by probing the physical, which is always a mistake.

This curiosity with hymens has continued down to the present day, but in this ancient story it is not received well. Salome reports that "my hand falls away from me in fire." She prays and her prayer is heard. An angel appears with the instructions for all healing. "Take up the child and this will save you," the angel says. The implication of the story is clear: Doting on the mechanics of miracles leads to destruction; embracing the living Christ brings life.

So, a child has been born whose ultimate energy is divine creativity, who brings the stillness of eternity into the frenetic rush of time. How we respond to him brings sadness or joy, and digging into his physical origins will bring us to a ruin that can only be healed by communion with his living presence.

What "historically reliable facts" do we need to know?

Meditating
on the Host

I was in a church and had just knelt down before
the Blessed Sacrament exposed in a monstrance
when I experienced a very strange impression.

You must, I feel sure, have observed that optical illusion which makes a bright spot against a dark background seem to expand and grow bigger? It was
something of this sort that I experienced as I gazed
at the host, its white shape standing out sharply,
despite the candles on the altar, against the darkness of the choir. At least, that is what happened to
begin with; later on, as you shall hear, my experience assumed proportions which no physical anal-
ogy could express.

I had then the impression as I gazed at the host that
its surface was gradually spreading out like a spot of

oil, but of course much more swiftly and luminously. At the beginning it seemed to me that I alone had noticed any change, and that it was taking place without awakening any desire or encountering any obstacle. But little by little, as the white orb grew and grew in space till it seemed to be drawing quite close to me, I heard a subdued sound, an immeasurable murmur, as when the rising tide extends its silver waves over the world of the algae which tremble and dilate at its approach, or when the burning heather crackles as fire spreads over the heath.

Thus in the midst of a great sigh suggestive both of an awakening and of a plaint the flow of whiteness enveloped me, passed beyond me, overran everything. At the same time everything, though drowned in this whiteness, preserved its own proper shape, its own autonomous movement; for the whiteness did not efface the features or change the nature of anything, but penetrated objects at the core of their being, at a level more profound even than their own life. It was as though a milky brightness were illuminating the universe from within, and everything were fashioned of the same kind of translucent flesh.

From *Hymn of the Universe* by Pierre Teilhard de Chardin,
(© 1965 in the English translation by William Collins Sons & Co.,
Ltd., London and Harper & Row Inc., New York, pp. 47-48).

Spirituality is a hot topic. It's talked about in the workplace, in healthcare, in teaching in sports. It is even being pushed in churches, synagogues, mosques and temples! At the moment, anything labeled "spiritual" is enjoying cultural currency.

Many critics call spirituality a Jello word—incapable of being pinned down. Or a chameleon word—taking on the color of whatever environment it finds itself in. Or a vague word—pointing to the soft stuff that "hard" people who make "hard" decisions in a "hard" world sneer at. Or a vanilla word—avoiding the intellectual and moral rigor of words like faith and religion and theology. Or a snake-oil word— the province of sideshow gurus trying to attract the gullible. Or a sharpie's word—used by those trying to get an edge over someone about something.

The critics are correct...and more.

Still, spirituality is the word of choice used by those of us who have become suspicious that there may be more to human life than is obvious. Most of us have little doubt about the physical dimensions of our lives. (If we are tempted to discount our materiality, a rap on the elbow quickly brings us to our senses.) Also, the social dimension of our lives is never far from our minds. We operate within family and interpersonal networks, we have roles, responsibilities, jobs, economic locations, mortgage payments, and assigned places in society and religion. And we are psychological beings who discover through introspection our individual personality traits, mental tapes, emotional triggers, and unconscious influences.

But are physical, social and psychological traits all there is to life? Do these three aspects of the human condition tell the complete story of our strivings? Or is there something else, something we call the spiritual realm?

Some of us are suspicious that there is. We suspect there may be an invisible, not-material reality that permeates the world. Teilhard de Chardin's story, "Meditating on the Host," does not seem so far-fetched to us. We think that maybe he is one of those mystics who sees things that are really there but that the rest of us just cannot quite grasp. In the story, the host—the Eucharistic presence of Christ—expanded to fill the whole world. As it did "the flow of whiteness enveloped me, passed beyond me, overran everything. At the same time everything, though drowned in this whiteness, preserved its own proper shape, its own autonomous movement; for the whiteness did not efface the features or change the nature of anything, but penetrated objects at the core of their being, at a level more profound even than their own life."

Spirit may be a reality that can enter into everything there is and yet not displace anything of that into which it has entered. Or maybe spirit is a reality already in everything as both its foundation and its destiny. The expanding host of this story could be the same reality Jesus talks about in the apocryphal Gospel of Thomas: "Split a piece of wood and I am there. Lift up a stone and you will find me."

Lao Tzu, the ancient Chinese spiritual teacher, said it this way:

> The Spirit of the Fountain dies not....
>
> Lingering like gossamer, it has only a hint of existence.
>
> And yet when you draw upon it, it is inexhaustible.

The spiritual dimension of life is subtle. It does not easily appear on our radar screens. It is as thin as gossamer. When we draw upon it, however, we find that it is abundant and inexhaustible, a limitless loving energy bent on human fulfillment.

This is what we suspect: A spiritual reality whose nature is to give itself permeates us and the entire cosmos. All we need to learn is how to receive the gift. So we investigate anew all the religious traditions, including those of our childhood, asking them to dust off their spiritual treasures. We become interested in beliefs, stories, practices that put us in conscious contact with this divine reality. In all this, we recognize the pitfalls and accept the risk of appearing (or even being) silly.

The Monk Who Wrestled with God

The ascetic was curled on the ground. He had raised his head, and I was able in the half-light to make out his face as it gleamed in the depths of unutterable beatitude—hairless, with sunken eye sockets, gnawed away by vigils and hunger. All his hair had fallen out, and his head shone like a skull.

"Bless me, Father," I said, bowing to kiss his bony hand.

For a long time neither of us spoke. I kept looking greedily at this soul which had obliterated its body, for this was what weighed down its wings and kept it from mounting to heaven. The soul that believes is a merciless man-eating beast. It had devoured him: flesh, eyes, hair—all.

I did not know what to say, where to begin. The ramshackle body before me seemed like a battlefield following a terrible massacre; upon it I discerned the Tempter's scratches and bites. Finally I gather up courage.

"Do you still wrestle with the devil, Father Makarios?" I asked him.

"Not any longer, my child. I have grown old now, and he has grown old with me. He doesn't have the strength.... I wrestle with God."

"With God!" I exclaimed in astonishment. "And you hope to win?"

"I hope to lose, my child."

From *Report to Greco* by Nikos Kazantzakis, (© 1961 by Helen N. Kazantzakis, English translation © 1965 by Simon and Schuster, New York p. 222).

I read this vignette many years ago in Nikos Kazantzakis' mythic autobiography, *Report to Greco.* It has stayed with me for two reasons. The first is: I do not like it. The second is: I do like it.

What I do not like is the characterization of the relationship between the body and soul, flesh and spirit. All the soul wants to do is escape. "I kept looking greedily at this soul which had obliterated the body, for this was what weighed down its wings and kept it from mounting to heaven." In this tradition, since soul passionately seeks its non-earthly destiny, it renounces the things of the flesh, especially food and sex. Therefore, the spiritual path is an endless wrestling with the devil, who tempts us into satisfying our bodily appetites.

This temptation is deep. In the crucifixion scene of Kazantzakis' *The Last Temptation of Christ*, Jesus falls into a reverie on the cross. He dreams he has settled down with Mary Magdalene and sits on a porch watching his grandchildren play. Jesus revives from his dream and realizes he is still on the cross and has not given in to the seductions of the earth. He has remained faithful by rejecting the last temptation—domesticity. As with the ascetic in the story, all the earth is a weight on the wings of Jesus' spirit, a prison to be broken out of.

But what if spirit did not want to break loose from earth? What if spirit yearned for the earth, yearned to suffuse and elevate flesh? What if the goal of the spiritual life was not bodiless union with a transcendent God but the incarnation of God in the world? As John Tarrant suggests, "Secretly, spirit wants embodiment; wants to sink down and be mortal, to bleed, to struggle with high blood pressure and menstrual cramps and cold toes." What if the passion of spirit is not to escape but to embrace?

This theme has emerged recently in a number of "angel" movies and television shows. They begin with guardian angels doing their jobs overseeing events on earth. Their lives are clear, passionless and detached. Then one of the angels begins to envy the chaotic but exhilarating lives of the humans. He or she falls in love with one of his or her charges and then figures out a way to leave the angel realm and enter the mortal and struggling world of the human. Then the real wrestling begins—angelic love becoming earthly commitment.

What I do like about the mini-story of the man who wrestled with God is the last line. The ascetic does not hope to "win" his wrestling match with God. He envisions "losing." What this means to me is that he wants to surrender into the ultimate Mystery that sustains and transforms all reality.

We resist this handing over of life. We know that at the end of our lives, we must pray the prayer of Jesus: "Father, into your hands I commend my spirit" (Luke 23:46). However, we fear losing control. We think that the moment the ego lets go is the moment we lose ourselves. Instead, it may be the very moment we discover ourselves.

The self that we will find is an identity intrinsically related to God. We will no longer be a separated self, spending our energies on strategies of promotion and protection. We will have an inner sense of being at home—even in the flesh the ascetic is so suspicious of.

When we "lose" our wrestling match with God, we can finally look out at the garden we were given to till and plant the seed we have discovered in our heart. The separated self that has lost its wrestling match with God becomes part of the divine adventure of the transformation of the earth.

The Mothers at the Grotto of Notre Dame

(As told by Mary Murphy)

My mom and dad are from Ireland, and I grew up listening to the Irish Hour and Notre Dame football on the radio every Saturday. This story took place at the Grotto of Our Lady at Notre Dame.

When I was a kid, we never could afford to go to Notre Dame. Now I go there regularly, but I'm old enough to stay at the elder hostel on campus. One afternoon, I rode my bike down to the Grotto, and I was sitting there on the bench looking around and feeling a little melancholy. I saw a lot of young people and thought to myself: I'm staying in the elder hostel now.

The Grotto is a place where when you go to it you kind of remember where you were last time you were there...and the times before that. I was looking at the candles and thinking: "I wonder what stories are behind those candles, what people had on their minds when they lit them, what was coming from their hearts?" I was getting more and more maudlin, to tell you the truth. I really missed being there with my young children. I mean I really missed it. I yearned to be a young mother again.

Then I saw a young mother coming down the path, pushing a baby in a buggy. She had three older kids with her. The mother sat down with the baby, and the other kids went right to the candle stand behind the railing and lit every single candle!

I was just sitting there and I wanted to be young again and be able to do that with my children. I had a flashback to the early sixties, when my friends and I all had a bunch of kids and no money. We didn't go anywhere... not even to fast food restaurants. But being "Notre Dame crazy," my husband Jim got tickets to the blue/gold game one year. We packed everybody in the yellow station wagon with stroller and playpen and the lunches and Kool-Aid and went to the game. It was a great game, and afterwards we all went to the Grotto.

This is what I pictured as I sat there, wanting that moment back. My kids had said, "Mommie can we lights a candle?" And I had said, "Nope, no candles. If one of you light a candle, then you'll all have to light a candle. You kids think money grows on trees.

Aren't you ever satisfied?"

I had said all that stuff and hadn't thought of it again until that moment. I was getting really emotionally upset and finding it hard to handle. I left the Grotto and had to walk the bike back to the hostel. I could hardly see because of the tears in my eyes.

A couple of days later, I went back to the Grotto. I was sitting trying a little contemplation, and when I opened my eyes I saw another young mother with two young boys. This mother was very agitated. It was a very hot afternoon, and she was all sweaty. Her hair was pulled back and her two little boys had black tee-shirts on and they kept wiping the sweat off their faces.

I had the feeling that this was the woman's first time at the Grotto and she really didn't know about "Grotto stuff." She looked around at the reverence of the people and all the candles and people praying and she wanted to do the right thing, so she told her kids, "Shhh, shhh, shhh, kneel down, kneel up straight..." and all that.

She was trying to take a picture, so I went up to her and said, "If you'd like, I'll take a picture of you all together." She said that would be nice and asked where they should stand. I said, "I have an idea, why don't you stand behind the altar? There's a big insignia in front of the altar that says 'Notre Dame,' and the kids can pretend they're saying Mass."

So they all went behind the altar and I took their picture. I could tell the woman wondered who I was.

She came back and kind of looked at me. I gave her the camera and she thanked me, then she hesitated and started away. Then she turned back to me and asked very innocently, "Can we light a candle?"

And I said, "yes."

That's the story, but it really was a profound experience for me, because I suddenly realized that I was the first mother who let her children light all the candles, I was the second mother who wouldn't let her children light any candles, I was the third mother who asked permission to light the candles, and I was the fourth mother who gave permission to light the candles.

I realized that we are all mothers, and that we are even more than mothers...all the time.

Mary Murphy told this story at a workshop on theological reflection. It engaged everyone, evoking both laughter and tears. The storyteller's reflections at the conclusion were satisfying and turned the sparse recital of events into deeper meanings while leaving even those meanings open to greater mystery.

With the squint eyes of a teacher I saw this story as an illustration of how experiences told in story form generate many meanings, yet none of the meanings substitute for the narrative. In other words, a story cannot be dismissed once one meaning or many meanings are derived from it. This is a great and subversive learning, especially for people educated to think that ideas are the highest form of human perception. Once you have the idea, they think, the rest can be jettisoned. The story of "The Mothers at the Grotto of Notre Dame," however, has a depth that remains—even after it has been mentally mined.

Here is an example of what I mean. A psychologist friend and I were once teaching a class together on the psychology and theology of the stages of life. He was explaining to the class Erik Erickson's theories of ego development. At one point, he quoted Erickson as saying the life cycle was both "gratuitous and relentless." One of the students asked what that meant.

My friend explained that "gratuitous" meant we are constantly offered certain possibilities and invited into life in a certain way. For example, we are presented with the tasks of identity, intimacy, generativity, integrity, etc., at each stage of life, whether we ask for these opportunities or not. We either freely accept the invitation or we do not, but if we do not then the life cycle becomes "relentless." It does not give up until we have worked through its agenda.

I immediately associated the ideas of gratuity and relentlessness with the Christian emphasis on forgiveness. There are urgings in the human heart to redo the past, to reconcile with what has been alienated. It is part of the gracious and freely offered activity of God. If this invitation is spurned, however, God finds another and more enticing way to relentlessly promote reconciliation. Human resistance does not have the power to block the inventive inroads of the divine. "Gratuitous and relentless" is a way of talking about redemption.

"The Mothers at the Grotto of Notre Dame," however, raises the ante on this classroom question-and-answer exercise. It is not a tale of redemption, of finding a way to redress the past. It is a tale of sanctification, of bringing all experiences into oneself and reconciling them in a series of ever higher realizations. Mary sees that she is all the mothers—not pitting one against another, not prizing one and denigrating the other, but allowing all their truths to be seen and appreciated. Then she takes another leap and realizes that "we are all mothers, and that we are even more than mothers...all the time."

This is what I mean about the power of stories. Where the psychologist and the theologian have an insight and stop there, the storyteller offers a holy communion that is inclusive of whomever and whatever will enter.

Could it be that in the intricacies of our days and nights we are being pursued relentlessly by a gracious Power offering us—gratuitously and relentlessly—a consciousness spacious enough to hold all we have been, all we are, and all we will be?

Is this what Jesus means when he says, "Not a hair of your head will perish" (Luke 21:18)?

My Father's Wealth

I was sitting in class on a hot September Saturday afternoon in 1959 when a lightbulb went off in my brain. I was eighteen, and—yes—it was a Saturday and I was in class.

You see, the school I went to was a high school seminary. We seminarians went to class on Saturday and had Thursdays off instead. According to the wisdom of the time, the point of this was to keep us boys separated from the shenanigans—from football games to dating—that were sure to happen on Saturdays. But being boys first and seminarians second, most of us spent most of the Saturday class time scheming about how to get *out* of class.

When the lightbulb lit, I suddenly saw a clear way out. In my mind, the Saturday doors of the school had just been flung wide open.

The movie *Ben Hur* had just been released and was getting rave reviews. More importantly for my purposes, the Catholic Legion of Decency had not condemned it. I had heard that Christ himself even made a cameo appearance. It was, therefore, perfect for seminarians.

The movie was playing downtown in the evenings, with matinees on Saturdays and Sundays only. There were no matinees scheduled during the week. Why not, you ask? Because there was no one to go to a movie during the week. Most people were working, and their kids were in school.

Ah, I thought, there are 948 boys who are *not* in school on Thursday afternoons. Perhaps the theater could be persuaded to have a special matinee on one Thursday, and the high school seminarians could all be persuaded to buy tickets and go to it. And I could do the persuading.

But what, you ask, does this have to do with getting out of class on *Saturday?*

I'll tell you. Every fall, the school had a "mission drive." This was an effort to raise a substantial amount of money to support the efforts of Catholic missionaries in foreign countries. It was a big deal in the seminary, and each classroom competed against the others to raise the most money. The winning classroom received an award.

One Saturday off.

The lightbulb shone in the darkness, and the darkness could not overcome it. I would convince the theater to have a special Thursday matinee showing of *Ben Hur.* I would buy the tickets from the theater for, say, one dollar each and then sell them to all my Thursday-off-with-nothing-to-do fellow students for, say, $1.50 each. With a turnout of 600—not unimaginable if you knew seminaries and seminarians in those days—I could make a profit of $300 for the missions. This would put my class over the top. A free Saturday was in the making.

Now, I have been told that some theologians of the Middle Ages thought part of the bliss of heaven was seeing your enemies in hell. This, I am sure, is poor theology. But certainly part of my motivation in coming up with this plan of genius was knowing that my friends in other classrooms would be in school some Saturday in the near future, while I and my fellow classmates would be out in the "world" that day.

So, I went to the theater that was showing *Ben Hur* and was directed to a very small office with a very big man in it. He oozed over the side of his chair like a melted cheese sandwich. He was smoking a cigar. "What do you want, kid," he snarled. "I ain't hiring."

I told him my plan.

"I ain't Catholic, kid," he said in a decidedly more friendly manner, "but I'll do it." He paused. "Of course, I'll need $600 up front. I gotta have some assurance."

I went back to school and sought out the priest in charge of the mission drive. I told him about my idea and how much it would raise for the mission drive. Then I came to the punch line. "Father, I need

$600 up front."

He looked at me for a long while, then he laughed. "I can't do that, Jack. It's too risky," he said.

I was despondent. I went home to talk to my father. Now, my father was a cop. We did not have a lot of money. I told him what I wanted to do and said, "I need $600."

"So do I," he said. But he gave me the money.

My surefire plan proved to be surefire. All the seminarians came to the Thursday showing of *Ben Hur*. My classroom won the mission drive. I paid my father back in six weeks—with no interest, of course. And I added "wheeler and dealer" to the growing sense of who I was.

And on a Saturday in early November that year, I sat in the bleachers of a high school football game of some non-seminarian friends of mine and practiced being in heaven.

Coda

It is now my father's eightieth birthday party in 1992. There are fifteen of us gathered at a restaurant. I am sitting next to my father. He is lifting a drink to his mouth with both hands. The drink is shaking slightly.

He puts the drink back down and looks at me. "Remember the time I lent you the money?" he asks.

We had not talked about that since 1959, but I knew exactly what money he was talking about.

"Yes," I answer, wondering what had brought this on.

"Did you ever think I wouldn't give it to you?" he asks.

"No, Dad," I reply, "I always knew you would give it to me."

"Funny," my father says, "so did I. I always knew I would give it to you."

In **Kitchen Table Wisdom,** Rachel Remen has a brief reflection called, "The Meeting Place." It begins with the story of a doctor who suddenly dies of a massive heart attack. For almost a year afterward, people come and sit in the doctor's waiting room. "At first, I would worry that they didn't know about Hal and I would have to tell them," the author writes, "but they all knew. They had just come to the place where they had experienced his listening, his special way of seeing and valuing them, just to sit there a bit."

We do well to revisit the places and times that we meet one another, the wheres and whens of the human condition.

I look at this story of my father and myself as a

memory of meeting, a recollection of a time we both recognized the truth of our closeness. There was a serendipity about it. Nothing was planned. We had not spoken about that incident with the movie in over thirty years, and this story was not one of those that had ever been recalled and retold when the "gang" would gather.

Dad's question came out of nowhere: "Did you ever think I wouldn't give it to you?" It was only then that I looked into my heart and memory and realized that I had *always* known he would give me the money, and I told him so. He then told me he always knew he would give it to me, too.

Father and son met, as only fathers and sons can. There had always been some silent assurance between us, and when it came into awareness—even years later—we recognized the connection, the simple fact that we came as a pair.

Of course, "My Father's Wealth" is a story about love, done in a typical male indirect way. It even occurred through the medium of money, the traditional male path of either generosity or greed.

No matter how it happens, however, there is something profoundly right, something full circle, about the meeting of parents and children as adults. Perhaps it is that the biological bond is completed by a personal and spiritual coming together. Perhaps there is so much nervousness and edginess in the relationship between parent and child that any real and unfeigned uncovering of love—even one that is a surprise to both parties—is a relief. Both my father and I could answer his question the same way in complete honesty, and the result was the revelation of an inner sameness, the sharing of the unsaid perception that we would always be there for one another.

It is important for parents and their adult children to know that. Allan Patton wrote a story called *Too Late the Phalarope.* It was about a man who never knew if his father loved him. As a result, the man's life never had the character and integrity it needed. Then one day, he and his father were bird-watching. Together they spotted a phalarope, a rare wading bird with webbed toes. This joint activity brought father and son together and revealed a rough love for one another that neither had been able to express. It was "too late," however, because the son had already strayed down dangerous paths from which he could not retreat.

In her stunning poem, *The Visitor,* Mary Oliver relates a similar experience. Her father visits at night and knocks wildly at the door. (I take this to be a dream or imagery for a mental process.) For a long time she does not answer, but when she does she looks into her father's blank eyes. "I saw what a child must love/I saw what love might have done/had we loved in time," she writes. The biological fact of their relationship was not completed in spiritual communion. The result is always sadness.

I have a suspicion that memory may be a culprit in all this. As Rachel Remen points out, we can go back to the *places* we have met. It may be more difficult to go back to the *times* we have met. I have no desire, for example, to return to the restaurant where my story's brief and symbolic conversation took place. But I host the time in my memory. I work at keeping it alive. I tell it, and now I have written it in a book.

Without cultivation, experiences fall out of memory. With some inner discipline and direction, however, we can recall and relish the surprising revelations of love that occur even in the off-hand moments of our lives.

My Mother's Best Putt

"Well, we did it," my teacher announced one day in May when I was in eighth grade. "We've finished the work for the year. Now we can have fun." We still had three weeks of school left, but Sr. Rosemary had whipped us through the second semester in record time and we had completed all the assigned material. "Now we can have fun," indeed.

Unfortunately, fun for Sr. Rosemary was a never-ending series of spelling bees ("Don't forget to repeat the word before you try to spell it"), geography quizzes ("What is the capital of Nigeria?"), and speed math ("All right, when I say 'go,' turn over the page and solve the problem. The first one finished, raise your hand"). Sister loved intellectual contests of all types—usually with the boys pitted against the girls.

Gender wars started early.

I felt all this busy work was really stupid. And I told people so—especially my mother. Those were the days when kids went home for lunch, and as I ate and my mother did things around the kitchen I complained vociferously and daily. My mother was—as usual—firmly on Sr. Rosemary's side.

"Why do you think it's stupid?" she would ask.

"Because it is," I'd reply. Did I have to explain the obvious?

"Well, it's only three weeks. Offer it up," she suggested.

Now, "offer it up" was Catholic code for "suffering can't be avoided, so you might as well get something good out of it." Rather than endure meaningless suffering, you could "offer it up"—usually for the "poor souls in purgatory." The idea was that you could gain merits by bearing suffering without complaint and then transfer the benefit to others who needed spiritual help. And nobody needed more help than the poor souls.

However, this redemptive use of my pain did not interest me. I continued my lunchtime assaults on Sr. Rosemary. Several times, my mother warned me that she didn't want to hear any more about the matter, but I kept it up.

One day, after a morning of supposedly "fun" quizzes, I launched a frontal attack on the "stupid" way we were wasting time. I was sitting at the table eating a sandwich, and my mother was washing some dishes. She had her back to me, but I noticed her shoulders suddenly arch and move up around her ears.

I knew I had finally gotten to her! She was now as angry at me as I was at Sr. Rosemary. Although I realized I was about to get "blasted," I felt a sense of triumph.

But then my mother's shoulders relaxed. Without turning around, she said, "It'll just take me a minute." She went into her bedroom and came out wearing a sweater. "Down in the basement," she ordered.

I wanted to ask what was going on, but for once in my young life I thought I had best keep my mouth shut.

In the basement, my mother pulled out her golf clubs. "Let's go," she said.

Totally confused, I picked up my own clubs and followed behind her. I was having trouble fathoming what was happening. It *looked* as if I was skipping school to play golf—with my mother, no less. She was playing the person feared by every Catholic youth of the time: she was being a "bad companion," luring me into wickedness.

We lived only six blocks from Columbus Park, a nine-hole Park District course. It cost a quarter for kids and seventy-five cents for adults to play. As we were walking over to the course, my mother chatted away about this and that, but she did not say one word about school or quizzes or Sr. Rosemary or what we were doing. I kept quiet, waiting for a shoe to fall somewhere.

On the fourth hole, my mother was about to putt out. She had about a four footer. I was holding the flag and waiting. She looked up from the ball and said, "We won't tell anybody about this."

Then she smiled.

Then she made the putt.

Kids pushing their parents' buttons is a national pastime. They all do it, and I suspect that one of the reasons is they are so good at it. Every child is part bulldog. They can "hang in there" with a single theme forever.

Of course, there is no talking to them rationally about the underlying issue. The key to driving any parent crazy is for the kid to repeat "It's stupid" or some such phrase over and over again. That was my strategy in this story from my childhood. Usually, the parent will finally explode and threaten or actually deliver a punishment. Then the adult will go into a room, close the door, and wonder just what kind of parent he or she is becoming (and why the firm resolution not to get caught in this particular trap is constantly being forgotten).

A major moment in every parent-child blow-up is when the parent manages to silence the kid with some variation on the classic retort, "Because I'm your mother" or "Because I'm your father." The child walks off mumbling, a seeming loser but actually a secret winner because he or she has managed to reduce the parent to his or her level. This is no small accomplishment, especially since both parent and child have played out this scenario many times before.

This reminds me of a story about Galileo. Under threat of punishment by the Church, Galileo had been forced to publicly reject his empirical observation that the earth moves. But as he walked away from the Grand Inquisitor after delivering his recantation, Galileo mumbled under his breath, "It still moves." It is the same with kids. As they sulk away from the fuming parent, they mumble, "It's still stupid."

"What did you say?" the parent demands.

"Nothing," answers the child.

Galileo would approve.

In this story, however, my mother doesn't lose it. Although I batter her every day with the same complaint, she never blows up. She comes close! Her shoulders rise to her ears as she listens one more time to my bellyaching. But something happens inside her that turns the situation around. It is what happens inside her that is "my mother's best putt."

In spiritual literature there is a lot of talk about contemplation in action. The project is how to stay recollected in the midst of activity, how to stay centered in the swirl of events. The greater the chaos around us, the easier it is to lose our sense of ourselves. We merge with the cacophony outside and become one more victim of outer forces—a plaything of circumstances. We become reactive, shining examples of stimulus and response run amok.

Spiritually mature people, however, manage an inner distance that gives them the freedom to respond differently—free to go against the grain, free to swim against the currents rather than be pulled along by them.

In my own struggle with this spiritual task, I have noted several stages of development. The first is what I call "the realization of redoing." Redoing means that you have lost it. But now you think better of it and realize that you can seek out the person or people (or kids) at whom you blew up. You redo what happened and—hopefully—come to a better outcome. In this scenario, the parent goes into the child's room to talk again, to redo the "blow up" into a "calm down." The mother or father realizes that nothing is written in stone. Everything can be rewritten. Even God wrote the ten commandments twice (check it out in Exodus). Getting comfortable with a life of redoing is a first step on the spiritual road to freedom.

The second stage of spiritual development is "the realization of pausing." Here, when you feel yourself losing it, you pause. I was told of a doctor who disciplined himself to stop a moment before he entered the room of each patient. During this short pause, he recentered himself and reminded himself that this next person was not just one more cardiac problem but a human being like himself. This moved him to a level of freedom to respond to the person, not just the disease. When my mother's shoulders arched to react, her soul paused. She was not going to respond in kind. And thanks to this "realization of pausing" she found another way, a way not predicted in parenting manuals.

The third stage is called "going without while remaining within." This is the ability to act in the outer world without losing our inner centeredness. It is said of Wisdom that "while remaining in herself, she renews all things" (Wisdom of Solomon 7:27). This is a paradox. I take it to mean that we tap into creative forces and see possibilities we would otherwise miss only by going within ourselves and that we will be successful only when we act from this inner space of recollection.

It is not that my mother did the ethically right thing by taking me golfing. She did, rather, the healing thing, the action that recognized my pain and gave me the power to live with it in a better way. The next day, I went back to Sr. Rosemary's "fun" without complaint.

Redoing, pausing, going without while remaining within—this is a spiritual path parents may understand and practice. Still, if you ever think you are making progress, just have your son or daughter say "It's stupid" to you forty-five times. After you have gone ballistic and are sitting on the edge of the bed wondering what went wrong, you will realize that the true inner essence of every spiritual path is perseverance...and humility.

The Nun Who Missed the Consecration

(As told by Sr. Georgene Wilson)

This happened about twenty years ago, just so you know I've changed. The particular event happened on a first Friday. Remember those nine first Fridays we made in order to make sure we would have a priest present when we died? That is the background for this story.

Often when I would go to church there would be anger inside of me because some of the presiders would pray the liturgy in less time than it took the elderly to walk to church. I get mad when things are more important than people. But this particular time Fr. Clem had Mass, and Clem must have been over ninety-nine years old. The best thing about Clem was that he would say, "Theeeee Loooooord beeee wiiiiith youuuu," and somehow you felt the energy of the Lord coming through.

So I was pleased that Clem was presiding at the liturgy until it came time for the homily. He said that because it was the first Friday in June he was going to do the Litany to the Sacred Heart, the Novena for the First Friday, and the Novena to St. Anthony. My mind wandered somewhere else. The next thing I remember was Margaret, who had come to church with me, poking me and asking, "Was there a consecration?"

"I don't know," I answered, "I buzzed out."

Margaret said that Clem had gone from the "Holy, Holy, Holy" to "Through Him and with Him and in Him," missing the consecration completely.

So as the time for communion came around, I said to myself: "That's not Jesus!" So I sat in the pew until Fr. Conrad came out to help Clem because there were so many people in church. Conrad went to the tabernacle and got the ciborium out with hosts that had been consecrated the day before. I don't remember thinking, but I do remember my body getting up and going in Conrad's line.

As I was walking back from communion, however, I thought: "How do I know that Clem didn't say Mass yesterday and forget the consecration then, too?"

So I sat down and started thinking some good thoughts, like: "What makes Jesus come, anyway?"

Over the long haul, that experience has changed my life. But the rest of the story is about how fast we can lose those kinds of insights.

After Mass, one of the little old ladies who always came to church tapped me on the shoulder and said, "You're a sister, aren't you?"

"Yes, I am," I replied.

She asked, "Did I receive communion?"

Now, all the woman wanted to know was whether or not she had broken her nine First Fridays. But I said to her, "What line were you in?"

You had to have been there. Every aspect of this story depends on a knowledge of Catholic life and theology in the Fifties. The catalyst of "The Nun Who Missed the Consecration" is an elderly priest saying Mass. These men are legendary in Catholic circles. One reportedly wore a hat at the eight o'clock Mass each morning because the sun filtered through the stained-glass window in such a way that it got in his eyes. Then there was the old-timer who mistook a round piece of cardboard for one of the hosts in the box they came in. When the time came during Mass to break the host, the priest discovered what it was and blurted out, "This darn thing is cardboard." (Legend has it that the congregation dutifully responded, "Amen.")

In "The Nun Who Missed the Consecration," Fr. Clem apparently skipped the consecration completely. This is no small lapse. Most Catholics believe that the words of consecration change the bread and wine into the body and blood of Christ. (The theological term for this is "transubstantiation.") Without these words, the hosts are just pretty bland bread. With the words, the love and power of God in Christ is received in the mouth and resides in the heart of the communicants. Hence the nun's dilemma: If Fr. Clem had missed saying the words of consecration, then under this theological world-view she and the rest of the congregation would not really be receiving communion at all.

In another twist of Catholic practice, however, Fr. Conrad had taken hosts from the tabernacle that had been consecrated at another Mass. If you got in his line, you wouldn't have to worry...or would you? What if those hosts had been consecrated at another Mass—perhaps by the same Fr. Clem—and the priest had missed the words of consecration then? The nun suddenly realizes that the hosts in Fr. Conrad's line might be frauds too!

What raises the stakes considerably in this story is the fact that all this happen at a "First Friday" Mass. If you went to Mass and communion on the first Friday of nine consecutive months, the devotion promised that a priest would be present at the time of your death. The priest would be available to hear your confession and you would enter eternity with all your sins freshly forgiven, thereby definitely avoiding hell and leaving open only the possibilities of heaven or—worst case scenario—purgatory.

So you see that—in the minds of many in the congregation that day—the drama of salvation and damnation was being played out as a comedy of errors.

The nun in this story is Sister Georgene Wilson, O.S.F.. She told this story in a workshop on theological reflection. We were discussing how people's theologies change under the impact of new thoughts and experiences. In particular, we were focused on how deeply entrenched our existing theological ideas and perspectives can be. Even when we question them and even after we begin to envision new formulations that are more adequate and life-giving, our old beliefs hang on.

This was the context of Sister Georgene's story. As she tells it, in the midst of all this inner panic about whether or not she had received a consecrated host, she is visited by a "good" thought. "What makes Jesus come, anyway?" she asks herself. "That experience," she tells us, "has changed my life."

But not immediately. There will have to be more reflection and more experience for that change to happen completely. For the time being it is an opening, but it is an opening that is able to re-close, an insight that is able to fade fast. And it does just that. Her marvelous last line to the woman concerned about whether she had broken her string of consecutive First Fridays, "It depends on what line you were in," is a testament to bulldog theologies that will not let us go easily.

When Sister Georgene delivered this punchline, all the participants in the workshop broke up. There were waves of laughter. People were howling. We had to take a break.

I felt the laughter was salvific. We humans live on the boundary of time and eternity, and we are severely tempted to solemnity as a way of life. We try to cut deals with the divine as if God was a rug merchant, and we take our scheming seriously. When our conniving is brought out in the open, as it is in this story, we see ourselves in a new way, a way that forces us to laugh at ourselves.

And in the aftermath we hear a quiet voice tell us, "There is only one line."

"Scaring Ain't So Bad"

"It was a long time ago, but I still remember it," said the old man as he closed his eyes to help sharpen his memory.

"It was late in the afternoon. A terrible storm was brewing. The sky was low and dark. I was out in the field. It was no place for a nine-year-old boy to be, so I made for an old shed on the farm where we kept tools and such. But I didn't make it before the storm hit.

"Fierce winds, pelting rains, lightening, thunder—I could barely see. I finally found the shed. Once inside, I crouched in a corner, sitting on some rolled-up rope.

"The shed was old, and the wooden slats had separated. When lightening hit, it sent shafts of light streaking through the cracks. The darkness in the shed would light up and then go dark again. It was like someone was standing in the room and turning a light switch on and off.

"Suddenly the door of the shed swung open. A massive, bearded man in drenched clothes burst inside and shook himself like a dog. Then he saw me, crouched in the corner. He looked back out the open door at the storm and then back at me. He yelled in a loud, deep voice, 'Ah, boy. He's trying to scare us today.'

"Well, that did it. I was already wet, cold and frightened. The last thing I needed was this giant of a strange man bellowing at me. I started to cry.

"The man came and sat down next to me. Then he took his fist—it was the size of a sledge—and slammed it into my shoulder. I could feel his breath on my face. 'Scaring ain't so bad, boy,' he said. Then he laughed."

This story was told at a workshop in Ireland in response to my request that the participants "Recall an experience that has influenced your faith." I had defined faith as basic attitudes toward God and neighbor, and I was looking for experiences that were formative of those attitudes. The man who told the story ended with "That experience has stuck with me."

In a theology class back in the states, I recalled the story and the wonderful way the man had told it. An irritated student piped up, "I'm tired of people talking about faith and avoiding the 'God' word. Faith is about God. Where is the 'G' word?"

The student was right about one thing. The word "God" does not appear in this story. The narrative lacks an explicit reference to the divine. But there is something about the man's experience and his story that invite a theological interpretation. His tale both expresses and evokes religious feelings, felt perceptions of the larger reality within which "we live and move and have our being" (Acts 17:28). Certain experiences trigger religious feelings. This story is about storm and shed and a strange and tense human encounter. Through it all, however, is not the larger mystery of people, earth and God being revealed? Although the story is about concrete particulars, we sense in them the presence of the Whole.

The boy is so frightened by the largeness and unpredictability of the world that he cowers in a corner. Suddenly, he is confronted by a still more frightening human figure. The older man knows terror and the source of terror. "He's trying to scare us today, boy," he says. Yet the man also knows a power beyond terror that allows him power over it: "Scaring ain't so bad, boy." In the lightening processes of human communication—swifter but less showy than the lightening that flashes outside the shed—the man mediates a salvific mystery to the boy. There is a reality that does not do away with terror but allows us to confront it and, through steadfast acknowledgment, overcome it. Mystery is not just revealed, it is revealed as the active encouragement of human hope.

Still, I'm reading between the lines. There is no explicit God talk in "Scaring Ain't So Bad." I suggest that on the level of lived experience this is perfectly fine. At a more refined level, religious language is used more frequently and freely, and everyone who speaks about spiritual matters unwittingly becomes a theologian and eventually dives into the different and difficult rules of God-language. But in storytelling it is appropriate and theologically justified to hold back on the "G" word. God talk communicates most powerfully when it knows its place and time, and its place and time is at the end, when there must be an almost reluctant acknowledgment that no other word can tell the complete truth of our experiences.

When the student registered her complaint, I was reminded of Flannery O'Connor's characterization of a woman in one of her short stories: It seems that the word "God" embarrassed the character the way the word "sex" had embarrassed the woman's mother. Now, this embarrassment might have been because the woman "lacked faith" or was one of those no-nonsense people who—like the doubting St. Thomas—has no time for anything that cannot be seen and touched. On the other hand, the woman's awkwardness might have been the result of keen theological intuition.

When we use God talk, we often give the impression that we know exactly what we are talking about, almost as if we are pointing our finger at someone. God is an invisible being or person who can only be seen through the eyes of faith. When the eyes of faith see God, the tongue of faith says "God."

The eyes of faith have 20-20 vision into the spiritual world, but it is not quite as simple as that. This normal understanding is also a misunderstanding. Kierkegaard once remarked that God is not "a great green bird." That is, divine reality is not one more object of perception—even an invisible object. God is not one thing within the created world; God is the source of the created world. What should cause us embarrassment is to speak about God as if we know what we are talking about.

What then is God talk about?

When we see a bird in flight or the rolling waves of the ocean or a mountain peak in the distance or two people holding hands or an old woman feeding pigeons in the park or a child asleep in a crib, and then suddenly through them the grandeur and misery of the human adventure breaks into our minds and hearts, God talk must enter the conversation. When bad fortune besets us or we do not think that we are going to be able to get out of a mess we ourselves have created or we are not able to face certain pain and difficulty that is awaiting us, and then suddenly we find the courage and support we need and realize that more is at work than ourselves and our friends, God talk must enter the conversation. When we see the evil and suffering of the world and sense an imperative coming from deep inside ourselves to do something about it, and then suddenly we are aware that we did not "make up" this drive within us but are responding to some reality that finds evil and suffering as offensive as we do, God talk must enter the conversation.

"God" should be an unforced word, emerging from our mouths only because of the fullness of our hearts. As Jesus pointed out, "It is out of the abundance of the heart that the mouth speaks" (Luke 6:45). The rationale for using the "G" word is that no other word will do. It should flow out of conversation for the purpose of discovering truth and meaning, not to prove orthodoxy or to "baptize" experience. If this is indeed the case, perhaps learning to talk *about* God is learning *when* to talk about God. (At least part of the injunction of the second commandment, "Thou shall not take the name of the Lord in vain," is that the "G" word should not be used as indiscriminately as ketchup on hamburger.)

Perhaps we should not talk about God until we have told a story—any story—in such a way that God is the natural and appropriate interpretation of what is happening. Modesty in God talk may be very revealing of the reality of God. "Scaring ain't so bad, boy," is the last line of an experience told in story form. An appropriate response for a biblically based people might be, "Even though I walk through the darkest valley, I fear no evil." Then, after the silence that is the prelude to all spiritual perception, the final truth of that storm-haunted Irish afternoon can be told: "For You are with me" (Psalm 23:4).

The Shepherd's Pipe

A villager who went to town every year on the High Holy Days to pray in the Baal Shem Tov's synagogue had a son who was so slow-witted that he could not even learn the Hebrew alphabet, much less a single prayer. And because the boy knew nothing, his father never brought him to town for the holidays.

Yet when the boy reached the age of thirteen and became responsible for his deeds, his father decided to take him along on the day of Atonement, lest he stay at home and, in his ignorance, eat on the holy fast day. And so they set out together—and the boy, who had a little shepherd's pipe on which he piped to his sheep, pocketed it unbeknownst to his father.

In the middle of the service, the boy suddenly said,

"Father, I want to play my pipe!"

The horrified father scolded his son and told him to behave himself. A while later, though, the boy said again, "Father, please let me play my pipe!" Again his father scolded him, warning him not to dare; yet soon the boy said a third time, "Father, I don't care what you say, I must play my pipe!"

"Where is it?" asked the father, seeing the boy was uncontrollable.

The boy pointed to the pocket of his jacket, and his father seized it and gripped it firmly. And so the hours passed with the man holding onto his son's pocket until the sun was low in the sky, the gates of Heaven began to shut, and it was time for the final prayer of the day.

Halfway through the closing prayer, the boy wrenched the pipe free from his pocket and his father's hands, put it to his mouth, and let out a loud blast that startled the entire congregation. As soon as the Baal Shem Tov heard it, he hurried through the rest of the service as he had never done before.

Afterward, he told the worshipers, "When this little babe played his pipe, all your prayers soared heavenward at once and there was nothing left for me to do but finish up."

From *Jewish Folktales* by Pinhas Sadeh, English translation
by Hillel Halkin © 1989 by Doubleday
(New York: Doubleday, p. 396).

When I read this succinct and moving story, as I have often done, I find myself pondering three spiritual truths. I am drawn to these truths because I do not know the whole of them. Their fullness is beyond me. So I return to them again and again, hoping more will be revealed to me.

The first truth is that there is a space within us deeper than the rational mind. The story characterizes the boy as slow-witted, unable to learn the language of worship. The mind is not his playing field. Yet he has a great capacity for worship that is symbolized by the shepherd's pipe. The symbol of the shepherd resonates throughout biblical literature. For example, Psalm 23 begins, "The Lord is my shepherd." David is remembered as the shepherd king, and Jesus is imaged as the good shepherd. The truth is that there is something within us that is a "shepherd's pipe"— an affinity with the divine, a natural wellspring of worship.

Yet this dimension of the son is "unbeknownst to his father." The "father" aspect of all of us is somehow ashamed of this deeper place within us. We would rather leave it at home. We fear that if we play the pipe we will be prone to make mistakes and break religious law. When the pipe emerges in the story, the father scolds and suppresses it. The spiritual task is to loosen the grip the "father" in us has on our inclination and ability to produce divine music. W. B. Yeats expressed this tension thus:

> God guard me from those thoughts men think
>
> In the mind alone;
>
> He that sings a lasting song
>
> Thinks in the marrow bone.

The second truth is that the shepherd's pipe will not be denied. There is something in the worship setting that calls to this deeper part of us—to the shepherd's pipe we each possess. This call overrides even the stern propriety of the father. "Father," the boy declares, "I don't care what you say, I must play my pipe." There is a necessity to praise God in us, a necessity that arises from the center of our being. Playing the shepherd's pipe is beyond obligation and respectability. The entire congregation will be startled by our music, but we are under the influence of a power that demands to be unleashed.

Prayer comes from many places. From our sense of imperfection we pray, "Help us, Lord." From our calculating minds we pray for guidance and insight. From our anxious hearts we pray for serenity. But the prayer of the shepherd's pipe is not *for* anything. It comes from our very being, from the sheer, unadulterated fact of existence. When Psalm 148 implores mountains and hills, fruit trees and cedars, wild animals and cattle, creeping things and flying birds to praise the Lord, it is asking for nothing less than for a song of being—the song that is played on the shepherd's pipe.

The third truth is that the shepherd's pipe attains its goal. It carries all the other prayers—prayers from real but lesser places in ourselves—to heaven, and it does so just in time. "The sun was low in the sky, the gates of Heaven began to shut," the story says. This is the last-ditch prayer, so to speak. It is the one that redeems the strenuous effort of human worship and makes liturgy itself superfluous. The Baal Shem Tov himself declares, "When this little babe played his pipe, all your prayers soared heavenward at once and there was nothing left for me to do but finish up." The shepherd's pipe summarizes, and ends, and in a way transcends the service.

Why is the prayer from the shepherd's pipe so complete and whole that nothing more is needed? So often, prayer begins with a sense of a missing God who has to be contacted and called upon. Our earthbound imaginations can construct only an absent reality who has to be summoned to pay attention to our considerable needs. The prayer of the shepherd's pipe, however, starts from divine presence. The boy senses divine energy pulsing in all things and is stirred to create music as his response. His prayer is less desperate and more playful than the adults around him. His prayer trusts and dances rather than cowers and pleads. It goes beyond "God out there and me here" thinking. Instead, it moves to the beat of the universe, the rhythms of the immanent God.

The prayer of the shepherd's pipe is not the type of prayer that waits for an answer. It *is* an answer—an answer to the exuberant presence of God welling up within us. It is a prayer that is complete and whole from the beginning. Or, as the Hebrew Scriptures put it, "Then I was beside him, like a master workman. I was daily his delight, rejoicing before him always, rejoicing in his inhabited world and delighting in the human race" (Proverbs 8:30-31).

In the Book of Proverbs, these words are ascribed to Wisdom herself. They also aptly apply to a boy who was "so slow-witted that he could not even learn the Hebrew alphabet, much less a single prayer."

The Shoelace

I n a moment of madness, I agreed to do a series of workshops on storytelling in Ireland. On the sleepless plane ride to Dublin, I pondered the real folly captured by the phrase "bringing coals to Newcastle." What idiocy was I undertaking—telling and talking about stories in the spiritual home of storytelling?

But the people were gracious and forgiving, and the humble truth soon became evident. I was there to learn, not to teach.

On the first day, I sat in a small group as a woman of about seventy-five told a story from her childhood. This is her story, flattened by print and my memory lapses, but impoverished most of all by the absence of her wonderful, soft, lilting voice.

"I was one of fourteen children," she said, "and my mother tried to put order in everything that had to do with our brood. Every Sunday we would walk to the church about three miles away. But before we set out, there was a home ritual every bit as set in its ways as what the priest did at Mass.

"There was only one mirror in the house, and my mother would stand in front of it. Then each of us would queue up and pass between my mother and the mirror. As we did, she would straighten us up and comb our hair. After this combing we could go out and play. When everyone was done we would gather and walk to church.

"One Sunday, I was about third in the queue. My mother looked down the line and saw that my little sister did not have a shoelace in her shoe. My mother looked at me and said, 'Go back and get your sister a shoelace.'

"But I did not want to lose my place, so I didn't budge. When my turn came, I stepped between my mother and the mirror. My mother said nothing. She simply combed my hair and off I went to play.

"I came in a little while later. My little sister—the one without the shoelace—was between my mother and the mirror. My mother bent down and took a shoelace out of her own shoe and put it in the shoe of my little sister. When I saw this, I went into the back of the house and got a shoelace. I came out and knelt at my mother's feet and put the shoelace in her shoe. As I did this and while she was combing the hair of my little sister, she reached down with her free hand and stroked my hair."

The woman stopped telling her story and looked

down. The people in the group said nothing until one man asked, "Are you done?"

She nodded. Then the man began to tell one of his stories.

After the session, I was walking around outside when the woman who had told the story walked by. I stopped her and said, "Your story blew me away."

"What?" she asked, and I realized that my "Yankism," as they called them, was causing her bewilderment.

"It was rich and moving," I explained. "I don't know what it means, but I was moved by it."

"It was stupid," she said. "I shouldn't have told it."

"No," I replied. "We are all better for having heard it."

"Thank you," she said, and then she walked on.

Coda

While I was conducting the workshops, I would pass the long, civilized Irish afternoon breaks sitting under a tree smoking a cigar. On the fourth day, the woman who had told the story approached me.

"Where is your cigar?" she asked.

"It's in my room," I answered, "but I am too tired to go get it."

"I noticed you didn't have one, so I bought you a

cigar," she said. She handed me a cigar.

"Thank you," I said.

I looked down and fiddled with the cellophane wrapper. When I looked up, the woman was gone. As I am smoking the cigar—thinking of nothing in particular—it suddenly dawns on me: the cigar is the shoelace, the cigar is the shoelace.

During the next session, I saw the woman seated in the back of the room. As soon as I was finished, I pushed through the crowd and found her. I loomed over her and said with way too much enthusiasm, "The cigar is the shoelace, the cigar is the shoelace!"

She looked up at me and stuck out her chin. "I know that," she said. She looked down and then looked back up at me. "It was a pact with my mother," she said with emotion. "It was a pact with my mother."

And as she said this, she hit her heart twice.

In his book, *One Rose, One Bowl,* John Stevens tells a Buddhist story that also revolves around shoelaces: "Once his brother asked Ryokan to visit his house and speak to his delinquent son. Ryokan came but did not say a word of admonition to the boy. He stayed overnight and prepared to leave the next morning. As the wayward nephew was lacing up Ryokan's sandals, he felt a drop of warm water. Glancing up, he saw Ryokan looking down at him, his eyes full of tears. Ryokan then returned home, and the nephew changed for the better."

The nephew in this story changes without words and without reprimand. Something mysterious happens in the lacing of the shoes, in the feeling of warm water, in the glancing up into the tearful face of the boy's uncle. The story does not tell us what that "happening" is. The inside of Ryokan and the inside of the nephew are not divulged. What we see is a silent, symbolic communication, and we are told that this encounter initiated a change for the better in the nephew.

One feature of this communication is the lacing of sandals. In spiritual literature, this is an activity that is imaginatively developed in many ways. In some traditions, a disciple approaches a teacher and asks, "May I watch you tie and untie your sandals?" This is code for, "May I apprentice myself to you and learn what you know?"

However, learning from a spiritual teacher entails more than appropriating information. It means learning to participate in the inner life of the teacher. What we can assume is that somehow the nephew entered into the inner life of Ryokan and learned something of tremendous importance. To find out what that something is, we would either have to inter-view the nephew or Ryokan or both, extrapolate what happened from our own experience, or have a sudden insight into the spiritual dynamic hidden beneath the surface of the action.

In the Irish woman's story, we have the same situa-tion. There is a silent communication between the girl and her mother that forever changes the life of the girl. The fact that a shoelace is in the center of the story indicates that a spiritual learning is hap-pening, that an exchange of life energies is going on.

It is important to note that reprimand has been by-passed. The mother could have rebuked her daugh-ter for disobeying and not getting the shoelace. In-stead, the mother takes the shoelace from her own shoe and puts it in the shoe of her younger daugh-ter. This selfless act by her mother, which the story-teller saw clearly, breaks through to her and opens up a level of life she had not previously seen.

The storyteller finds a shoelace and kneels to put it in the shoe of her mother, who strokes her hair as she laces the shoe. Something very powerful is go-ing on. As I told the woman, it "blew me away." Still, as I also told her, I didn't know what it meant. The communication between mother and daughter was silent and symbolic.

Fortunately for me—and for you, perhaps—as the workshops continued over several days at least part of the meaning was revealed. I usually smoked a cigar during those leisurely afternoon breaks, and the storyteller noticed that. One afternoon I did not have my cigar, and she noticed that, too. She bought me a cigar and gave it to me. She is, therefore, a person who notices what is missing and supplies what is absent.

Many other people saw me smoking my cigar day after day, and some of them saw that I did not have a cigar on that particular day. But it did not register with them, or at least it did not occur to them to try to remedy the situation. This Irish woman, however, perceived what was not there and was keen to do something about it. For her, my missing cigar was her mother's missing shoelace, and her gift of the cigar to me was her kneeling to put the shoelace in her mother's shoe. Invisibly, her mother stroked her hair as she gave me the cigar.

Although this was a revelation to me, it was not news to the woman. She already knew what was going on, and she understood the depth of it. "It was a pact with my mother," she said. Then she hit her heart twice to show me where the pact had been made—in the spiritual center of her being, in the place where her mother still lives.

This storyteller's life unfolds out of the perceptions formed in her on that long ago day when she laced the shoe of her mother and her mother's spirit flowed into her. Call her what you will—by her baptismal name, by her social role, by her ethnicity, by her personality type—but do not forget her secret identity, bestowed in that silent flow of spirit: She is the "one who notices what is missing and supplies what is absent."

Both as individuals and collectively as a culture, we are very interested in how people develop. We contend that people change because they are convinced by reasoning or threatened by consequences or conditioned by environment or shamed by disclosure. We call upon these theories because we seek to influence others, to pass on values, to seize "teaching moments," to reinforce preferred behaviors. There is probably a piece of truth in every theory of human change and development, but perhaps we should also make room for the mysterious—for those unplanned, silent, symbolic communications where spirit flows from one person to another, establishing pacts that endure forever.

The Stillborn's Baptism

The group of chaplain residents in our clinical pastoral education center had been asked to present a pastoral event that seemed to be full of meaning and in some way evocative of theological reflection. The event that Doug shared involved a baby who had been stillborn. The parents wanted to have a memorial service in the hospital chapel. Doug tried in vain to get a more experienced chaplain to officiate at the service because he felt he did not know what to do.

When Doug found that he would need to do the service himself, he quickly prepared some things to say. However, when the nurse brought the stillborn baby into the chapel where he and the parents were, Doug found that he could not say what he had planned to say.

"All I could do was stand there and cry," he said.

Not knowing what to expect, Doug was not surprised when the nurse handed him the baby to hold.

"I want you to baptize my baby," the mother said.

Doug nodded, but he saw no water with which to baptize the baby. Almost without thinking, Doug took a tissue, wiped the tears from the eyes of the parents and his own eyes, and touched it to the baby's head and whispered, "Nicole, I baptize you in the name of the Father, Son and Holy Ghost. Amen."

Some theorists think religion is born and sustains itself around "limit" experiences. That is, when we reach our limits, we also instinctively reach beyond them. We pray, so to speak, at the edges. Some of those edges are the experiences of birth, death and helplessness. At these times, we either thank or implore the larger Mystery that is the permeating context of our lives. We also, as in "The Stillborn's Baptism," create rituals to help us relate to these limits.

Birth, death and helplessness have come together in this story to create an edge we all fear. Doug, the student-chaplain, is preparing to enter his limit region. He knows this is a realm where experience is needed, but he has none and cannot find a more qualified minister. So he tries to fortify himself with words and phrases he has concocted in his mind, but he is unable to speak them.

At our limits, words we fabricate are not worthy. They cannot measure up to the pain and loss we are encountering. We are reduced to silence, which on one level is speechlessness but on another is the only appropriate form of presence. Here we honor Wittgenstein's famous dictum, "Whereupon one cannot speak, one should be silent." We do not try to fill the abyss with human stammerings.

A more experienced chaplain—one who had not reached his or her limit—might have hardened his or her heart enough to get through, might have thrown words at the darkness. Doug, on the other hand, teeters on the edge. He turns the tears of helplessness into the water of hope. The words he employs, however, are not his own. He reaches for ritual words, words that have been sanctified by centuries of use. "Nichole, I baptize you in the name of the Father, Son and Holy Ghost. Amen." Who knows what these words mean in this context?

I never know what to say on the edges, when my own limit is reached, when I cannot actively help but am reduced to simply being there. My outer silence is always the sign of an inner emptiness. It is not that I do not have faith. It just seems that whatever words I can muster would just trivialize the *mysterium tremendum et fascinans* (the overwhelming and fascinating mystery) that we encounter at those moments. When I look inside for words, all I see is darkness covering a bottomless space.

This is why I have come to appreciate one of the functions of religious rituals. They are a home built in the land of limits, a house constructed on the edge of experience. We do not have to build ritual from scratch, create it from whole cloth, spin it out of our innards like a spider. It is there for us to use when speech and gesture desert us, when our grieving and fearful souls need a voice and cannot find one. In effect, we borrow the collective voice of our people, handed on to us in the form of ritual.

We must inhabit all our experience. We have no choice; escape is impossible. Sometimes, however, all we can supply are the tears. Our rituals must supply whatever meaning or hope or consolation is possible. Mystery lies beyond our limits, where human tears are transformed into baptismal waters.

The *Szabo*

A man came to a *szabo*, a tailor, and tried on a suit. As he stood before the mirror, he noticed the vest was a little uneven at the bottom.

"Oh," said the tailor, "don't worry about that. Just hold the shorter end down with your left hand and no one will ever notice."

While the customer proceeded to do this, he noticed that the lapel of the jacket curled up instead of lying flat.

"Oh that?" said the tailor. "That's nothing. Just turn your head a little and hold it down with your chin."

The customer complied, and as he did, he noticed that the inseam of the pants was a little short and he felt that the rise was a bit too tight.

"Oh, don't worry about that," said the tailor. "Just

pull the inseam down with your right hand, and everything will be perfect." The customer agreed and purchased the suit.

The next day he wore his new suit with all the accompanying hand and chin "alterations." As he limped through the park with his chin holding down his lapel, one hand tugging at the vest, the other hand grasping his crotch, two old men stopped playing checkers to watch him stagger by.

"*M'Isten,* oh, my God!" said the first man. "Look at that poor crippled man!"

The second man reflected for a moment, then murmured, "*Igen,* yes, the crippling is too bad, but you know I wonder . . . where did he get such a nice suit?

We twist ourselves out of shape

in the mirror of others' eyes.

We parade for appearance,

   making alterations as we go,

presenting ourselves to the glass,

preening to please its empty power.

It is demanding.

Amputate an arm

   for those who cannot reach out.

Blind an eye

   for those who cannot see.

Stanch the flow of the heart

   to be loved by the frozen.

No sacrifice too great

to strut

a suit of our own making,

crippling us before God,

but dazzling in the darkness

of our own sight.

Naked, our only hope,

like Francis in the piazza of Assisi,

stripped of his merchant's clothes,

no cloud in the sky above him.

Two Brothers and the Temple

Two brothers shared a farm. One brother was married and had seven children. The other brother was single. They worked hard and the land was good. Each year the harvest was abundant, and each year they split the wealth of the land evenly. They gathered the perfectly divided grain into their separate barns and thanked God for his goodness.

One night the single brother thought to himself: "It is not right that we should divide the grain evenly. My brother has many mouths to feed and he needs more. I have only myself to look after. I can certainly get by with less." So each night the single brother would take grain from his barn and secretly transfer it to the barn of his married brother.

That same night the married brother thought to him-self: "It is not right that we should divide the grain evenly. I have many children who will look after me in my old age. My brother has only himself. Surely he will need to save more for the future." So each night the married brother would take grain from his barn and secretly transfer it to the barn of his single brother.

Each night the brothers gave away their grain. Yet each morning they found their supply mysteriously replenished. They never told each other about this miracle.

Then one night they met each other half way between the barns. They realized at once what had been happening. They embraced each other with laughter and tears.

On that spot they built the Temple.

This popular story from the Jewish tradition can be easily read on a social level. Each brother focuses on the needs of the other and generously gives from his own supplies to meet those needs. Therefore, neither's supplies diminish. Giving away does not deplete.

With the last line of the story, however, this lesson in social sharing takes a turn toward the spiritual and the sacred: On the place where they embrace, they build the temple.

There is a law in the spiritual life. Or, perhaps better said, in the spiritual realms of life there is a recurrent pattern of operations, a dynamic that appears again and again. In Christian spirituality, this law is expressed in one of the beatitudes in the Sermon on the Mount: "Blessed are the merciful, for they will receive mercy" (Matthew 5:7). Often this maxim is understood in terms of a three-party transaction. I show mercy to someone; God notices my merciful activity. Then sometime in the future when I need mercy, God remembers my giving of mercy and rewards my giving by showing mercy to me. God is the scorekeeper of the giving and receiving of mercy.

The giving and receiving of mercy, however, can be understood in a more dynamic way. The giving of mercy comes from the spiritual center of a person, the place where the person is connected to the Divine Source. This source is inexhaustible, without limit. Once released, it keeps on giving. This abundance of spirit is activated by the very act of giving it away. So, paradoxically, when love or compassion is shared, there is more love or compassion available for everyone—including the one who initiates the giving.

The opposite is also true. When spirit is hoarded, there is less of it. Holders may think that holding onto love or compassion insures that they will have what they need, but they have not reckoned with this strange law of spiritual living. Negatively stated, when you hold onto spirit, you lose it.

The reason we equate "holding" with "having" is that this is how physical and social laws work. If we have a house or a loaf of bread or a ticket to a Broadway show and give it away, we no longer have it. If we hold onto it, it is still ours. "Two Brothers and the Temple" will not let us go that way, a way we know only too well. The story suggests that resources are abundant and that rather than protecting what is "ours" we have to trust another dynamic. What is needed is for us to exercise the law of mercy from the spiritual realm in the world of our social relations. We have to incarnate spirit into society. That is why the temple is built on the place of embrace: The holy has transformed the divisive way we grasp and keep to ourselves the goods of the earth.

The practical in us cries out, "But this won't work." Yet the spirit in us quizzically observes how we cling to ways of behaving that are counterproductive and may even be killing us. My suspicion is that we will never commit ourselves to the "how" of social sharing until we have seen with steadfast clarity the "why" contained in the truth of spiritual giving.

Here is our choice: become a world of temples or a world of separate barns.

Credits

"The Cigar Smoker" from *The Spirit Master* by John Shea. Copyright ©
1987, 1996. "Two Brothers and the Temple" from *An Experience
Named Spirit* by John Shea. Copyright © 1983, 1996. Reprinted with
permission of Thomas More Publishing, 200 E. Bethany Drive, Allen,
TX 75002.

"The Grocer and His Parrot" from *Tales from the Land of the Sufis* by
Mojdeh Bayat and Mohammad Ali Jamnia. Copyright © 1994. Reprinted by arrangement with Shambhala Publications, Inc., Boston.

"Meditating on the Host" from *Hymn of the Universe* by Pierre Teilhard
de Chardin. Copyright © 1965 in the English translation by William
Collins Sons & Co. Ltd., London, and Harper & Row Inc., New York.
Used with permission of Harpercollins Publishers.

"The Monk Who Wrestled with God" from *Report to Greco* by Nikos
Kazantzakis, translated from the Greek by P. A. Bien. Copyright © 1961,
translation copyright © 1965. Reprinted with permission of Simon &
Schuster, Inc.

"The Shepherd's Pipe" from *Jewish Folktales* by Pinhas Sadeh. Copy-
right © 1989 by Doubleday, a division of Bantam Doubleday Dell
Publishing Group, Inc. Used by permission of Doubleday, a division of
Random House, Inc.

"The Stillborn's Baptism" from *From Ministry to Theology* by John
Patton. Copyright © 1990 by John Patton. Used with permission of
The Journal of Pastoral Care, 1068 Harbor Drives S.W., Calabash, NC
28467.

"The *Szabo*" from *Women Who Run With the Wolves* by Clarissa Pinkola
Estés, Ph.D. Copyright © 1992, 1995 by Clarissa Pinkola Estés. All
rights, including but not limited to performance, derivative, adapta-
tion, musical, audio and recording, illustrative, theatrical, film, picto-
rial, reprint, and electronic are reserved. Reprinted by kind permission of Dr. Estés and Ballantine Books, a division of Random House,
Inc., and Random House UK Ltd. (Rider).

Also from ACTA Publications

Christmas Presence
Twelve Gifts That Were More Than They Seemed
Edited by Gregory F. Augustine Pierce
Winner of a Catholic Press Association 2003 Book Award. This bestselling collection of stories about Christmas gifts that revealed the presence of God includes John Shea's "The Christmas Kaleidoscope." (160-page hardcover with gift ribbon, $17.95)

Hidden Presence
Twelve Blessings That Transformed Sorrow or Loss
Edited by Gregory F. Augustine Pierce
Twelve original stories about how grace can flow from sadness. A hopeful book for those who believe that God is with us, even in our darkest hours. Includes Joyce Rupp's "The Gift My Brother Gave Me." (176-page hardcover with gift ribbon, $17.95)

Gospel Food for Hungry Christians
Matthew, Mark, Luke and John
John Shea
This series of audio tapes offers a unique view into each of the four Gospels. It brings scripture, spirituality and theology together in new, refreshing and rewarding ways. (Four separate sets of six audio cassette tapes, $29.95 each)

The Man on the Ox and Other Tales
The Antique Watch and Other Tales
John Shea
Two separate video tape programs, each containing nine of John Shea's favorite stories told by professional actors, with commentary after each by Shea himself. (Two separate 40-minute VHS video tapes, $29.95 each.)

Available from booksellers or call 800-397-2282
(www.actapublications.com)